PURE
MIND
PURE
MARRIAGE

MICHAEL AND JUDI RYAN

ISBN 978-1-63814-212-6 (Paperback)
ISBN 978-1-63814-213-3 (Digital)

Covenant Books, Inc.
11661 Hwy 707
Murrells Inlet, SC 29576
www.covenantbooks.com

Marriage should be honored by all, and the marriage bed kept pure, for God will judge the adulterer and all the sexually immoral.

—Hebrews 13:4 NIV

CONTENTS

INTRODUCTION

THE DEVIL IS IN YOUR BED

So the great dragon was cast out, that serpent of old called the
Devil and Satan, who deceives the whole world... But woe to
the earth and the sea because the devil has gone down to you!
He is filled with fury because he knows that his time is short.
—Revelation 12:9, 12 NKJV

The devil is in your bed. He slithers in there every chance he
gets...unseen...undetected... secretly infiltrating your intimate
moments. That serpent of old, he is intent on defiling your sex life
and ruining those intimate moments between you and your wife.
He may have already done it. He has been successful in so many
marriages, robbing them of the joy sex is supposed to bring to married couples. Satan is the sworn enemy to every marriage intent on
honoring God and experiencing the blessings God intends marriage to bring. He is your enemy. He is your wife's enemy. He is the
enemy of your marriage.

To be sure Jesus was right to describe this enemy as the thief
that comes to steal, kill, and destroy. Stealing, killing, and destroying
are his goals for you—his ultimate battle plan for every area of your
life. This enemy is looking for any opportunity to accomplish his
plans in every aspect of who we are as God's people. This plan to
steal, kill, and destroy is just as true as it pertains to physical intimacy
in our marriages. Because this is a book about sex, we are going to

7

focus in on that specific area of marriage to expose the darkness of his schemes to the light of God's Word. It is the living and powerful Word of God which does that type of heart surgery to root out anything that the devil has planted there which accomplishes his plan to ruin sex for us. Once we have rooted out his lies, we can then replace them with thoughts and perspectives which honor God and bring the blessings of His kingdom into this extremely precious area of our marriages.

Let me introduce you to our theme verse for this book. It comes from the letter to the Hebrews, but it needs to be received as instruction to all of us as it pertains to our marriages.

> Marriage should be honored by all, and the marriage bed kept pure, for God will judge the adulterer and all the sexually immoral. (Hebrews 13:4 NIV)

There are many things this verse can teach us, but one of the most important is that sex and marriage are God's idea… God's plan. Therefore, because God planned sex and marriage, sex *in* marriage can and should be pleasing to God. Our marriage beds ought to be held in high honor and the purity of it should be guarded and cherished. God wants married couples to glorify Him in the expression of their sexual intimacy. This may sound like a strange statement to some of you, but it is true!

God invented sex. He invented the wonder and mystery and pleasure which can permeate the relationship between a man and his wife. God was the Originator of the act of marriage, "making love" as we may call it…a man "knowing his wife," as the Bible sometimes calls it. He intended sex to bring wonder, pleasure, mystery, and blessing to our marriages. As a matter of fact, when the blueprints for sexual expression were formulated in His mind, there was a specific group of people He had in mind: men and women who love Him and seek to glorify Him. It is those men and women who love and honor Him who have decided to enter into a lifelong covenant of commitment and companionship that God designed sex for. Who did God invent sex for? Christian married couples!

If that is the case, it stands to reason that married Christians are the group of people in the world who should be most blessed by it. Would it surprise you to know that this is exactly how things are?

A study done at the University of Chicago surveyed a large group of women that included various segments of culture to see just which "category" of women enjoyed sex the most. Most of the researchers envisioned that it would be the young, attractive, single women who enjoyed sex the most. However, the results were a bit different than the hypothesis! Their study showed that married religious women with more than three children were the most satisfied with their sex lives! Needless to say, the people who conducted the study were very surprised, and so is the rest of our culture!

Christian women enjoy sex the most? This was what God intended! Unfortunately, many Christian men have allowed the devil to deceive us and rob us of that reality. That which God has intended as a blessing and an adornment to Christian marriage for many of us has turned into a great source of frustration and conflict in our marriages. That which has been intended to unite and strengthen intimacy often divides and weakens our relationship. All the while the devil grins with a twisted smile, knowing that his plans have been successful once again. One more marriage robbed. One more married couple's intimacy killed. Another blessing destroyed. Another marriage bed defiled. Another marriage and another and another...

What are Christians to do about this? Are we to just succumb to the false notion that our bedrooms will be a constant source of frustration and division for our marriages? Is there anything that can turn things around, make it right, and kick the devil out of our bedrooms? Many Christians realize that sex in their marriages is not all that God intended it to be. They may also realize that the devil has gotten his scaly foot in the door of our sex life. But they may also doubt there is hope for that situation to change. Is there anything that can turn this around and make it right? Some may doubt it is possible, but the heart of faith answers that question with a resounding and hopeful "*yes!*" Look what God says in this verse in 1 John:

> The reason the Son of God appeared was to
> destroy the devil's work. (1 John 3:8b NIV)

Do you believe what God says here? Can the presence of Jesus in your marriage destroy the works and schemes of the devil? Can God undo what the devil has done to our sex lives? The answer is "Absolutely! Yes! Amen and amen! He can." Not only can He, but He *wants* to do it for you and for me! It is the reason He came: to do some demolition work where the devil has been doing construction (more like destruction) in your bedroom.

News flash! Jesus wants to do some demolition, and if you have ever undergone a renovation project in your home, you know from experience that remodeling can be a messy process! Construction sites are always messy when the demolition begins. However, when Jesus makes a mess, He always cleans it up nicely when He is finished. Jesus's "projects" always end up amazing in the end. But know this: the main area He intends to make a mess is with you! As a Christian husband, Jesus has some work to do in you. Because you are holding this book in your hands, it indicates to me that Jesus wants to begin His remodeling work in you. This book is written to Christian men and written with the purpose of uncovering, defining, destroying, and replacing the idol we have made of sex. This is not about your wife and her faults or shortcomings in the sexual department. This is not about helping her to change and think biblically about God's design for sex (even if that may need to happen). This is about opening the walls of your heart to discover the faulty wiring the devil has run that creates the short circuits in your bedroom. It is about pulling out that faulty wiring and letting the Master Electrician do His job of getting it right so we are not blowing fuses every time we try to plug in sexually. This is about *you* and letting Jesus search your heart for any idols that might be enshrined there concerning your perspectives about sex.

In the book of Judges, we come across a story where God intends to deliver His people from a pretty nasty situation. Israel's enemies were regularly invading their land to plunder and destroy. The end result of all this plundering was that God's people were impoverished and cried out to God for deliverance...and God intended to deliver them! The Lord chose a man named Gideon for the job. Though he did not necessarily seem like the best man for the job, He was God's man. In a little bit of a plot twist, the first job God gave Gideon was not to head off and fight off the enemy but rather to tear down and destroy his father's idols. The altar gets destroyed and Gideon offers a sacrifice to God where the old idols once stood. After the idol demolition and rebuilding of a proper altar, God brought great deliverance and peace to His people.

The situation for Christian husbands often parallels the story of Gideon. The enemy of their marriage is plundering and robbing them of the sustenance sex in marriage is intended to bring. However, there are idols present in their hearts: on the altar where God should be worshipped. They need to be torn down! Those heart idols are often the source of our frustrations and struggles, just as they were for Israel in the story of Gideon. Israel engaged in gross idol worship which lead to the constant raids from the Midianites. Those Israelites cried out to God for deliverance from their trials but got mad when the first thing God does is tear down their idols! However, for the deliverance to come, the idols had to go.

In similar fashion, we cry out to God for Him to deliver us from our frustrations in the sexual realm...to do something to solve the problems we experience in our marriage bed. All too often, we do not realize that the first step in that deliverance is some demolition work. He has some idols which have been set up in our hearts which need to be destroyed!

Idolatry was a consistent problem that plagued God's people throughout the Old Testament, so it should not surprise us to find it is to be consistent problem we still struggle with today. It has once been said, "The human heart is an idol factory."[1] Your heart is no

---

[1] John Calvin. Institutes I. 11.8.

different from others. There is no help found in denying that our hearts can manufacture idols. The real question is whether we deal with them properly when we find them there!

So…are you ready for Jesus to be the Gideon in your story? He is on the job with His sledgehammer in hand ready to destroy the work of the evil one. He is prepared to demolish the sexual idols in your heart and rebuild that altar properly so sex in your marriage can and will bring glory to God! Put on your hard hat and dust mask and get ready for some remodeling!

CHAPTER 1

FASHIONING IDOLS

Dear children, keep yourselves from idols.
—1 John 5:21 NIV

John the Apostle ended his first letter with an odd instruction: little children, keep yourselves from idols. It is not odd in the sense that being idol free is a good thing for a Christian to be. It is not odd in the sense that we know idolatry can have negative consequences. It certainly is not odd in the sense that we know God hates idolatry. However, it is odd in the sense that this command seems like it does not fit with the rest of his letter. It seems like a quick add-on at the end…kind of an apostolic postscript. "P.S. my dear friends, keep away from idols."

Whatever was the reasoning behind John adding this to the end of his letter does not remove anything from the importance of the command found in that verse. Idols are something we are to keep away from. Many Christians might say, "That should be simple. Any time I come across a little Buddha statue for sale in a store or at a garage sale, I just won't buy one. Easy verse to obey." It would seem so, if we think of idols as little statues sitting in shrines or on the mantle of our fireplaces. Not many of us are tribal people living in the jungles of Africa leaving little offerings at the altars of statues, praying that they give us good luck as we go out to hunt for food.

So it stands to reason that we might assume we will not be tempted much with idol worship. But I am not so sure it is that easy.

There is an interesting verse found in Colossians 3:5 NIV where Paul discloses a list of sinful behaviors which we are to put to death, sexual immorality, and evil desires and coveting and the like...and then Paul describes these behaviors as being idolatrous. Notice:

> Put to death, therefore, whatever belongs to
> your earthly nature: sexual immorality, impurity,
> lust, evil desires and greed, which is idolatry.

If nothing else, this verse teaches us that idolatry can be more than simply burning incense in a shrine or setting offerings before a statue. But even more than that, Paul is saying that the lifestyle which may include these types of earthly perspectives is, in effect, idol worship. The presence of one or more of these things: sexual immorality, impurity, lust, evil desires, and greed can reveal a heart which is governed by an idol. These are perspectives which our sinful natures develop in our hearts that amount to idol worship. Our flesh has the ability to take any good thing which our God has created and turn it into an idol. We can do it with money, wealth, and status. We can elevate any of our desires to a place of idol worship. Jobs can be idols, relationships can be idols, homes and possessions can be idols, even the desire to get married or have children or have a ministry could be idols. Humans have the inane ability to turn even the noblest of things into objects of worship. We do it very often, more often than we would care to admit.

Many men have done that very thing with sex. Sex can be an idol. I do not only mean having sex can be an idol, but our perspective about sex and the level of importance it has in our lives. Perspectives such as: what it is sex supposed to "look like," what I am supposed to feel when I am having sex, what is my wife supposed to feel when we are having sex, what are we supposed to say or sound like when we are having sex, even how often I think we should have sex can be influenced by an idolatrous perspective. We can assign a level of importance to sexual expression and fulfillment which give it entirely too much importance. Many different aspects of sexuality can be idolatrous in nature. In our hearts we can elevate sex to a level of importance which God never intended it to have. Our "image" of what sex should be like and do for us has become an idol for so many men…even Christian men.

Defining Idolatry

Before we go much further, it might be helpful to work at getting a good understanding of what the Bible has in mind when it speaks of an idol. What exactly is forbidden when we are commanded not to fashion for ourselves any idols? A good place to begin is with the commandment written in stone and delivered by Moses:

> You shall not make for yourself an image
> in the form of anything in heaven above or on
> the earth beneath or in the waters below. You
> shall not bow down to them or worship them.
> (Exodus 20:4–5a NIV)

In the second commandment, God describes the situation He is forbidding: the fashioning of idols. Notice that idols are something *we* fashion; *we* form them, *we* make them, *we* create them. We use something already created as a basis for our idols like the command says, "in the form of anything in heaven or on the earth or in the waters below," but *we* are the ones doing the creating. We take what God has created and we begin to imagine that thing differently; in our minds we give it different purposes. We give it attributes and powers it was never supposed to have. We think of the created thing as being able to give us something it cannot give us. We elevate something created by God to a height and importance which God never intended it to have over us. God sees Himself as being the All-Sufficient Provider for our lives, but we think this created thing can give us something which, in reality, God alone can provide. That thing or person or situation becomes so important that God gets displaced from His proper position in our lives and a created thing takes

His place. We start to serve that thing by giving it our attention and affection and our heart. We may have never intended to bow down to it and worship it, but that is exactly what eventually happens.

Let us not overlook this one crucial reality: when we fashion idols, we are doing it for ourselves. All idol worship is essentially self-worship! Notice the way this command begins, "You shall not make *for yourself*…" When we create idols, we have ourselves in mind. We look to that idol to give *us* something or do something *for us*! Our idols ultimately reflect ourselves and our selfish desires. This is one of the reasons idols form so easily in our lives…because we are self-focused and selfish. It comes natural to us. From the moment we are born we are naturally predisposed to focus on our selves. We need food; we need comforts; we need to feel loved and wanted; we have needs and we expect them met. If they are not met, we cry and carry on until they are. Self-focus comes naturally to us because it is a part of who we are. No one I know would hold that reality against a baby. A baby cannot live long in its own situation without the self-focused expressions that let others know it needs to be cared for.

But the question is: Do we ever outgrow the perspective of self-focus or self-centered or being selfish? The people in our lives sure hope so! Most of our sin issues are inherently linked to our failure to outgrow our own selfishness. All idolatry comes from our self-centered hearts, and all idols are made to fulfill a self-focused desire or longing.

How is this for a decent definition for idolatry?

> Anything, anyone or any situation we look
> to provide for us what God alone is supposed to
> give.

I know I am not the only one out there who has defined the concept of idolatry and I have found some other definitions that have been helpful for me in understanding and defining idolatry. Pastor Brad Bigney has defined an idol as "anything which captures your heart, mind or affections more than God." That is a helpful way to look at things. Has anything captured my attentions and affections more than they should? Is my worship of or desire for God displaced by the desire for this thing in my life? What is my heart focused on? Answers to those questions can help us uncover idols in our hearts.

Another helpful perspective useful in discovering if I have an idol in my life is by answering the following three questions:

1. Am I willing to sin in order to get this thing?
2. Do I sin as a result of not getting this thing?
3. Do I run to this thing instead of God when I am looking for refuge?

The presence of sin which is there on account of trying to get or not getting something could indicate that we have elevated a created thing to the position of something to be served or worshipped. After all, if we disobey God's commands on account of something we want, would that not indicate we value and serve that thing too much? This indicates we have inappropriately placed our attentions and affections on something God has created. We set aside service and worship of the One True God because of this "created thing." We are willing to sin to get it or sin if we do not. We run to this thing instead of God to give us the peace or rest or fulfillment which we should look to God for. We reveal by our actions that this thing or person or situation has become an idol. Many men have done this very thing with sex.

Has sex become an idol for you? Does it capture our attentions and affections more than God? Do we look to sex to provide us with something only God is supposed to? Many of us might initially answer those questions, "No. I do not think I have turned sex into an idol. I don't worship it." But let me ask those questions a little differently: Is your feeling of self-worth and fulfillment derived from the woman you sleep with, how well you perform in the bedroom, how enjoyable sex was for you or her, or even how often you make love with your wife? When sex is not all you may have imagined it to be, does it create a sinful response in your heart? Do you sin against your wife or yourself when you do not get sex when and how and how often you think you ought to? Answers to those questions may indicate more than we would like to admit about how a created thing (sex) has become far too important in our hearts and minds!

How Idols Develop in Our Hearts

Idols made of stone or wood are fashioned by our hands. They are literal, physical items that can be seen, felt, and handled. Idols of the heart are spiritual, internal, and developed in and by our minds and hearts. They are fashioned by our thoughts and desires. But do not be fooled... Just because they cannot be physically handled, they are just as real...even more so than the real ones! Our thoughts and perspectives are the most influential realities in our lives. They can shape and mold the way we behave in every situation we encounter. Even though our idols do not sit on a shelf or in a shrine in our homes, they are a more powerful force than we know. We do not see them, but they are always present. They are invisible influences ruining the things we touch. That is the way the devil likes it! If he can keep those idols hidden deep in our hearts, then they can be a tool he uses to manipulate and influence our lives, stealing and destroying without us ever being aware of what is going on.

Another truth we need to face is, whether we like to admit it or not, if there is an idol in our heart, we are a slave to it. All idols by nature are served and worshipped. They demand loyalty and obedience. They require service and worship. We bow down to what we elevate. We protect and cherish what we treasure. If we have placed a high value on something, it influences our hearts and lives. Jesus said it like this:

> For where your treasure is, there your heart
> will be also. (Matthew 6:21 NIV)

This is a reality we cannot escape or imagine does not apply to us. It is a maxim for everyone who ever lived, from the lowest to the greatest.

How Do We Turn Sex into an Idol?

When it comes to idols of the heart, or the "things we treasure," we are often unaware that we are fashioning them. They mostly are developed in secret...unnoticed and invisible. They get created slowly and methodically by our fleshly, earthly desires. They take shape as we grow and experience life. Life experiences come our way and our minds evaluate and think about what we experience. This is often an unconscious process which all of us engages in. We inwardly calculate to determine exactly how important what we are thinking about or experiencing is. We all classify and appraise and develop a personal system of values.

When it comes to sex, these realities are taking place in our hearts long before we even care about it. As small children, before we even understand what sex is, we are presented with data and information we are not mature enough to know what to do with. Thoughts or concepts we are too young to contemplate get presented to impressionable minds and we try to evaluate them. Our simple hearts absorb and "file away" images and thoughts in the file cabinets of our minds which get planted like seeds in the fertile soil of our immature and impressionable minds. Those seeds eventually grow to determine our perspectives about sex. Even when those icky and gross "other people" we call girls are not someone we care much about sexual perspectives are developing in our little heads.

If we give any serious thought to how the devil got into our bedroom undetected, we will find that his devious plan began long before we ever had a marriage bed to defile. He had infiltrated our intimate moments long before we ever had any. Through the years he has been stowing away his lies and deceptions in our thoughts and minds. His scheme began when we least expected...when we were little boys. His weeds were planted long before we even had any level of sexual interest in girls.

When it comes to how the idol of sex got fashioned in our heart, we must realize this reality. If we intend to pull this idol out by the root, we need to recognize and deal with how those roots developed. As we grow and mature from boys to men, there are different spheres of influence for our impressionable little minds. I have taken some time thinking about what the sources for where our ideas about sex could possibly come from while we are maturing, and I have boiled it down to five different categories. This is not because there are not more but because these are the main sources for our mental input while we are growing up. They are as follows:

1. Family
2. Friends/Peers
3. Entertainment/Media
4. Education
5. Pornography

Numerous books have been written on each one of these subjects which highlight the dangers and problems that each of these categories present. I do not intend to dig too deeply into each one of them but do want to briefly mention a few things about each of these categories to highlight how they can contribute to the fashioning of sex into an idol in a man's life. Just reading them, I am sure some of you have quickly connected dots in your own past where thoughts and perspectives about sex were forming during your experiences in some of those categories.

Another quick point to make about this list is that obviously, these sources of influence will differ for each of us and some of these categories may overlap in the way they came to be influences in our lives. For instance, the first time you encountered pornography may have been through a friend. Also, some of us may have received our education through our family on account of being homeschooled. But as it pertains to the general categories of influence, there is a good chance that each of these has been a factor in our development of perspectives pertaining to sex. It is also worth noting that some of these influences may have been stronger in some of our lives more than others. Young men who were exposed to pornography regularly may have been influenced by it more than a boy who only saw it once or twice. But the main point to make is this: our sources of information about sex can and do influence the way we think about it.

Family

It is an unfortunate reality in our culture that the family unit is not as strong as it should be. God Himself has placed a high value on families. It was His intention that the family would be the foundation for all societies, cultures, churches, and countries. Strong families create strong nations; weak families create weak ones. Homes where love, respect, honor, and unity are valued characteristics have an obvious tendency to create healthier children and produce more productive members of society. Homes where parents love each other and raise their children well strengthen individuals and, as a result, the culture around them. The opposite is true as well. Though there may be exceptions to the rule, broken homes produce broken people.

How people relate to others is conditioned in the home. How we get along with our brothers and sisters, how our parents related to us, how parents got along with each other...all of these experiences contribute to our development as we grow and mature. As we grow up, if we learn to communicate well, seek and give forgiveness, be kind and compassionate, and genuinely care about others, we have a foot up on life. We can also develop bad relational habits if those experiences taught us poorly. Our experiences and how we handle them combine with our personalities and have worked together to turn us into the people we are.

The family unit can also impact the way we think about sex. Each member of the family has a perspective on sex, which may be expressed in the context of us living together under the same roof. Children are much smarter than we might give them credit for. They are sponges, regularly taking information in and processing it. I think it was James Dobson that said it, "Values are mostly caught, not taught." I take that to mean children develop values as they pick up attitudes and perspectives on the fly. Random comments or actions register in their impressionable minds, and all the while, they are almost entirely unaware of the process occurring.

Think of all the ways the topic of sex could be addressed in the home. Let's start with the parents. There is a possibility that Dad and Mom could be openly physical in front of the children, hugging and kissing, holding hands, Dad patting Mom on the bottom as he walks by, intimate innuendos in their communication—displays that generally communicate the idea that sexual expression between a husband and wife is normal, healthy, and appropriate. Children in this environment would think this is the normal and natural way a man and woman relate in marriage. However, if Dad and Mom are very reserved and unexpressive physically, hush-hush about sexual expression between a husband and wife, and take a very hands-off approach to physical relationship, obviously a different perspective would be developed.[2]

Let's move to big brother or sister next. Do my older siblings ever express what they think about the topic of sexuality in the context of relating with the family? Of course they do! Do older siblings openly make comments about the opposite sex? "She's so ugly!" or "He's cute." Are they crushing on a celebrity or someone at school or church? Do either of them have a girlfriend or boyfriend? Do they express what they think makes a member of the opposite sex attractive? Does sister have a crush on a guy at school? Is brother taking a girl out on a date? Do they make fun of each other for liking someone? How does my sister dress, and does she wear makeup? Does Mom or Dad come down on her for the way she dresses or how much makeup she put on? Are they going to the prom? Are they jealous of their friends and their steady flames? There are numerous ways that ideas about the opposite genders relating to one another is expressed in the context of our families. So many different expressions that influence thoughts about the opposite gender!

And all the while there is little Johnny taking it in and trying to make sense of everything he sees and hears. What is important about this stuff? Are looks important? Is a nice body important? Is dressing this way or that way important? Is long hair or short hair important? Is it bad to have acne or greasy hair or big ears or a pointy nose or to

---

[2] At this point in our discussion, I am not trying to communicate which of those approaches to sexuality in marriage is right or wrong, or if one approach is better than the other. I am merely attempting to point out that the way parents express themselves concerning physical intimacy in front of children can and does impact the thoughts a child might develop about sex.

be too skinny or too overweight or big hips or to be too tall or too short? Is it good to have big breasts or big muscles or a nice smile or to be super smart or to be athletic or to have a nice car? What does my family think is physically attractive? It can be confusing or enlightening. What is a young boy supposed to make of all this?

One sure thing he does make of it is: *it is important!* My brothers and sisters seem to think so. Mom and Dad seem to make a big deal about it! And all along the way, little Johnny begins to understand and evaluate that these things are valuable. Guy-girl relationships are important, even from his little "I don't want to have anything to do with girls" perspective. It is all forming an opinion...a perspective or a belief system as the information comes in.

And then the extended family shows up. Family gatherings and holidays bring grandparents and aunts and uncles and cousins into the mix. They each have their own perspectives which they cannot help but express. The relatives see Junior playing with a girl outside and for some reason feel the need to ask if she is his girlfriend. Uncle Joe jokes around with his nephew, saying, "Hey, Johnny! Do you have a girlfriend at school yet?" Grandpa asks him, "Are there any pretty girls in your Sunday school class?" What is a boy supposed to think? Aunt Jane thinks having a girl as a friend is different than having a boy as a friend. Uncle Joe seems to be communicating that you are not doing well if you do not have a girlfriend. Grandpa thinks pretty girls are the important ones...and so they must be!

It should be obvious that such things can have an impact on the development of our perspectives concerning the opposite gender...guy-girl relationships. A young man who does not know what to think about a topic he is too young to seriously comprehend is developing a value system based on information he is receiving from his family. This mostly happens totally unintentionally, but it most certainly does happen.

This reality occurs the entire course of his life growing up. At times it is more specifically related to the topic of sex, and at other times there are only implications toward sexual concepts, but in every situation a boy is processing the data. Boys grow up to be men. That is the natural order of things! The ideas and concepts we develop when we are young become a part of who we are as we mature and the process of taking in and evaluating information about sex is happening the whole way. And here is the kicker: if Johnny is not processing the data in line with God's perspectives expressed in the Scriptures, he will ultimately make poor judgments and wrong assessments about that information.

There is only one way for us to keep our paths straight. We must not lean on our own understanding but in all our ways acknowledge Him (Proverbs 3:5–6). Our own understanding is flawed and bent. Flawed and bent is especially true for children. "Foolishness is bound up in the heart of a child…" (Proverbs 22:15a NKJV). And you can bet that if foolishness is the filter through which a child tries to make sense of his experiences, then his conclusions will be filled with error. This process I have been describing regularly happens absent of the influence of the Scriptures sorting out the data. Even Christian families can create an environment where the process goes unnoticed and therefore unaddressed in ways that miss out on helping Johnny evaluate everything properly.

Friends/Peers

Family is not our only source of information about sex as we grow. Our friends and peers can also be one of our main sources of information concerning sex. Peer groups and friends are one of the main sources of influence in what we believe about sex. This certainly would include our closest friends but definitely is not limited to them. A boy can have a best friend, and his best friend can influence his perspectives, but what about other kids he hangs out with? His best friend may have brothers and sisters that are part of the mix. What about other children at church and at school or on the sports teams he plays on or the programs he may be involved with? A boy will most definitely find himself in many situations outside the home and it would be naive for any of us to think perspectives that concern sex and girls do not surface in those settings!

Friends and companions are often the first people outside of our families that boys allow to have shape their values. Friends and companions are human relationships that inherently come with the power of influence. This means that who we hang out with could influence us. The Bible talks about this in Proverbs 13:20 NIV:

> Walk with the wise and become wise, for a
> companion of fools suffers harm.

There are two types of peer groups listed: wise companions and foolish ones. We can easily see this verse teaches us that both groups exercise the power of influence over their peers. The wise companion can influence their peer toward wisdom and the foolish one can lead them to harm. That is the way peer relationships are. There is no avoiding it. A person can be blessed or cursed by friends and peers. Their presence in another person's life could change them for the worst or for the better.

In the presence of their companions, young boys will often put their belief systems to the test. If they are formulating opinions about things, it is usually their peers that are the first people who hear about it. In the realm of thoughts concerning sexual matters, this usually begins small. It could be that they repeat a comment they heard or make a joke about a girl. Thoughts that are rolling around in their brains may rise to the surface when they are with a friend. A question might come up, such as, "What do you think about Sally? I heard she liked you." Little things that test the waters and let them know if it is safe to step in. And if the waters appear safe, then deeper thought can rise to the surface. Familiarity gives way to security and security can open the door to more intimate subjects being broached.

The older a boy gets, the more the topic may come up. Children are often experimenting with the dating scene much earlier than they ought to. Their peers present them with the notion that they should have a girlfriend and they decide to try it out. Her friends tell your friends that she likes you. You give her a piece of paper with the question on it: "Do you like me? Mark yes or no." She marks yes and boom! All of a sudden you have a girlfriend. (It was all so simple back then!) The next time there is a school function, your friends are encouraging the two of you to hold hands or kiss. Games like truth or dare and spin the bottle are popular among the youth! What is a young boy to do except put to the test what he has begun to believe? His inner thoughts concerning girls are given the chance to develop further or evolve into what he is now experiencing.

Inwardly, it is all exciting and new. At whatever age these types of experiences happen, they bring with them some newfound thrill associated with girls. Some boys wade into these waters before they have left grade school. Others have them in junior high or high school. It is a rare young man who makes it through the school age without being pushed in some degree into deeper waters with girls.

Along with these types of experiences, the thoughts and perspectives about sex are developing with them. And just as true as it was in our first category of our families, if these thoughts and perspectives about sex are developing in the absence of the influence of God's Word, then we are most likely getting the picture all wrong. The Scriptures keep us on the right path...the way that is pure.

Is it possible for a young man to navigate the waters of youth and friends and companions and end up thinking and believing properly? What can keep a boy from turning sex into an idol? Psalm 119:9 ESV sheds some light on that:

How can a young man keep his way pure?
By guarding it according to Your Word.

Figuring out the way on our own will not keep it pure. Only God's instructions in His Word gives us light and shows us the straight path. Sex is a topic that needs the protection that the Word of God provides in order to prevent it from going south and turning into an idol. Without it we end up suffering harm from our foolish companions and we miss out on the wisdom which may be found among the wise.

Education

Education has evolved a great deal in our country. What began being done mostly in homes and by families slowly moved into churches and Sunday schools and then to little one-room school-houses. Over time bigger buildings were constructed by towns and cities and states. Along the way, God and religion were given detention and suspensions and eventually got expelled from class. Some private and religious schools popped up here and there along the way, but by and by it has been our government which has willingly stepped forward to offer to educate our children for us. This summary of education in America obviously has a lot of blanks to fill in, but it explains the general process which has brought us to the modern academic situation.

Most of our children's peer interaction takes place in the context of school or school events. Riding the bus, walking the halls, sitting in class, and eating lunch in the cafeteria make up most of a student's school day. There are also sporting events, band, plays, clubs, yearbook, and dances which result in large amounts of time where children are in the presence of their friends and peers. We have already touched on the developmental influence that peers have on boys as they grow, but education also puts our children in the presence of adults who are purposefully there with the intent to mold and shape the next generation. Many teachers love the opportunity to forge the "bright young minds of the future."

Being a strong influence on the future of our country is a noble cause. Teachers have one of the toughest and most important jobs around. Children need to be shaped and molded! Nobody wants a world filled with adults who never outgrew their own immaturity and childishness. Nor do we want a world full of intellectually challenged grown-ups who cannot read, write, or do simple math. That would not be a great situation. However, when I bring up education as a category of influence on the development of the male perspective on sex, I do so with the knowledge that reading, writing, and arithmetic are not the only things that our schools teach our children. More that is taught then just the main subjects that dictate the class schedule. Yes, there is also science and history and the arts, but there is also a sexual education that takes place in our schools—a sexual education that is formal as well as informal. Teachers may have an agenda that is not spelled out in their itinerary and syllabus but regularly surfaces in class discussions and rationales.

Formally, sex education might take place in health class. When I was in school, that type of instruction was put off until high school when boys and girls were experiencing puberty and hormones and "really needed that information" to help them navigate the pitfalls of such an awkward moment in their lives. That may have been the reasoning behind the timing of that instruction back then, but today our teachers and administrators have chosen to move those discussions to younger and younger age groups. These days even kindergarten students are flipping through books with pictures and lessons about the birds and the bees.

Parents with children in the public-school system may or may not even be aware of this reality. They might be okay with it, or if they found out about exactly what is happening, they might be livid! And if they know that sex ed is occurring, they may or may not be aware of is that the information is not limited to just the biological elements that are inherently linked to the topic of sex. Today's sex education includes more than just body parts and their proper names and how they all work together to make intercourse possible. In our current public-school sex ed "classes," one can also expect to receive instruction that address beliefs on what is normal and appropriate, and even more pertinent to our discussion…what is right! For instance, they will answer this question for students: "Should you wait to have sex until after you get married?" Who knows the answer to that one? Would it be a surprise to any of us to find out most public-school sex ed teachers think and promote the concept that premarital sex is normal, healthy, and good? For most sex ed teachers, premarital sex is expected and encouraged as they stand before a classroom full of thirty to forty impressionable minds. If they deem students old enough or physically mature enough to have sex, they will hand out birth control as often as students want it, just to be sure that they can engage in sexual activity "safely." Not only normal… not only healthy…not only good…but their encouragement of it communicates to their students that it is also right.

You will not be surprised that teachers also have well-prepared answers to questions like, "Should sex only happen between a boy and a girl?" or "Is it okay for a boy to wear girl's clothes and think he is a girl?" The current academic answer to those questions is by no means in line with what the Bible teaches!

But answers to questions pertaining to transgender or homosexual activity does not end with whether it is okay or not. They also address what to think about people who do not think it is okay! What do we call people who think transgender people or homosexuals are engaging in sinful behavior? Are those people good or bad? Are they loving or not? Are they tolerant or intolerant?

Anyone with half a brain can see that boys' mind-sets and perspectives concerning sex can be seriously influenced by education. Influencing mind and thought and perspective is the entire purpose of education! Whatever subject we might be dealing with, education aims at transforming thought about it through providing our brains with information. Sex education void of God's Word and biblical boundaries is destined to develop thoughts and perspectives in its students which develop sexual idolatry. Any time we do not think biblically about a given subject, we will ultimately find ourselves in error about it. The Bible is the only source of truth. God's Word is the ultimate determiner concerning right and wrong, good and bad, spiritually healthy or unhealthy. And when a kindergarten-aged boy is taught the highest form of hate toward someone is to think someone is wrong about how they express themselves sexually, it forces them to accept all things sexual as normal, healthy, good, and right.

It is apparent that a mind-set open to anything and everything as good and right is easy pickings for the enemy of our souls. "If you don't stand for anything, you'll fall for anything" is how the old saying goes. Public-school sexual education sets us up to fall for anything.

Entertainment

There is no avoiding the obvious reality about our culture that we are a people who must be entertained. It is big business keeping the Western world's entertainment appetite satisfied. Movies, television, Amazon and Netflix Originals, YouTube, Snapchat, Instagram, TikTok, video games, free game apps on every phones and tablet… the list goes on and on and on because our appetite for entertainment goes on and on. We are a society immersed in our screens. I have not even mentioned what comes through our headphones and radios as we go about our regular tasks. It is almost as if even when we are supposed to be working, we must be entertained! Western society most definitely is a culture that loves pleasure just like 2 Timothy 3:1–4 warned us, that they would be "lovers of pleasure rather than lovers of God."

Our children love being entertained as much as our adults… maybe even more! It is an ironic situation that technology is better understood by our youth than our adult population. Grandparents asking their nine-year-old grandchildren to set up things on their phones or tablets or smart TVs is a regular occurrence in many families! This dynamic may have developed because of a few different factors. One might be that our youth have been targeted by industries as a serious source of revenue. A small amount of time observing television commercials around Christmastime will attest to this reality! Young children are a major target market. Not that children have a lot of money, but businesses know that parents will spend their money to keep their children appeased. The more entertained they are, the less of an inconvenience they can be to Mommy or Daddy. This reality might be the largest contributing factor to this situation! Many parents develop the tendency to use entertainment as their children's "babysitters," so to speak. If they need a break or want some peace and quiet or need to get some task done without being interrupted, a television or tablet or video game will keep a child distracted for a good long time! And sometimes, they think, "The longer the better."

The average number of hours a child will spend before a screen on a regular day varies on their age level but is somewhere between 6–7 ½ hours a day.[3] That number is rising every time we do research on it! That revelation about how much time a child spends on a

---

[3] "Screen Time for Children," SelectHealth.org blog, September 2018.

phone, a tablet, a computer and/or a television can be like having an epiphany. The implications of spending that much time doing something is incredible to contemplate. Seven hours a day is over 2500 hours a year…in front of a screen! Many developmental specialists promote the idea that what they experience in these hours may be having the most influence on the development of their beliefs and perspectives.

In the child-rearing community, there has been an ongoing debate over which has the bigger influence on kids: quality or quantity time. When it comes to entertainment, we see both things happening at once! Kids are doing what they like (quality) and they are doing it for long periods of time (quantity). The question many are asking is "How negative of an impact does seven hours a day in front of screens impact a child's development?"

Though I am an advocate for limiting the amount of time children regularly spend in front of a screen, let me address more pointedly the kind of information their minds are being inundated with during the time they are in front of a screen. What things do they see concerning our topic of sex? The scope of this book does not intend to go into great depth concerning every type of negative influence entertainment bombard a developing young mind with. That would require a series of books limited to that subject alone. But at least let me posit a few questions to give you a chance to think through what a child sees on those screens seven hours a day. In the entertainment that a child engages in (video games, TV shows, movies, cartoons, etc.), how do the women dress? Are they dressed in ways that communicate modesty or prominently display sexual features? Actresses in movies and shows, are they average women (speaking about physical attractiveness) or are they women who could pass as underwear models? In TV shows or movies which children regularly watch, is there ever any level of physical relationship between the guys and girls (i.e., kissing, making out, implication that they have slept together, or scenes where they sleep together)? Do the sitcoms or shows they watch ever present any idea of what married life is like? Is marriage presented in a positive light or a negative one?

As a man familiar with the type of entertainment our culture feeds us, you know the answers to these questions. You more than likely get my point. All those hours in front of a screen communicates certain things concerning sex and women to a young boy. They are developing thoughts that pertain to their perspective concerning sexual things. The enemy is whispering to them, "This is what women are like. This is what makes a woman attractive. Boy-girl relationships operate like this. This is what men think about women and sex. This is what you should think too." It would be foolish to think what or who entertains our children does not specifically influence their thoughts or perspectives about sex.

Pornography

The last category I have listed in the contributing factors which lead to fashioning sex into an idol is pornography. Though I have listed it last, it is certainly not least. I would contend that the viewing or use of pornography is the quickest way to pervert sex into an idol. Pornography is a problem in our society of epic proportions. This is such a major issue that we will need an entire chapter to address it!

CHAPTER 2

PORNOGRAPHY

*I will set nothing wicked before my eyes; I hate the work
of those who fall away; it shall not cling to me.*
—Psalm 101:3 NKJV

The cards are stacked against us. The table is run by the house and the old saying seems truer than ever: "The house always wins." A young man almost does not stand a chance against the devil's attempts to pervert God's design for sex.

Here is a frightening statistic to consider: the average age a boy sees pornography the first time is when he is twelve years old. Twelve! Obviously, this means some kids see it younger than that and some see it when they are older, but the reality is this: long before parents have taken the time to teach their sons about sex, the devil is already doing it for them! Pornography does more than just present you with something to look at or watch; it teaches you! It explicitly shows you how sex is "supposed" to happen. Right before your eyes, you have enacted before you exactly what sex is supposed to be like...how it is supposed to happen, what is supposed to sound and look like, and how gratifying it is supposed to be. And not surprisingly, if you're just a twelve-year-old boy without any guidance, you don't know any differently! You end up believing exactly what pornography "teaches" you.

My first encounter with porn was around the age of nine to ten. This was because a friend just accidently found a pornographic magazine in the ravine behind his house. My guess is that one of the neighbors had thrown it out with some trash and it was just lying there along with some old tires, a mattress, and couch. He was obviously curious after he came across it, like young kids can be, and flipped through the pages. He had never seen anything like this before and brought it home to show his brother and sister. The next day when my mom dropped me off to hang out for the day, he showed me too.

I cannot remember each and every picture we looked at, but I do still have some of them indelibly burned into my memory. I certainly will not describe it for you here, but if I needed to, I could. It is an odd thing that I can remember it so well. Come to think of it, though I have seen quite a vast amount of pornographic material in my time growing up, there are certain images I can still very vividly recall. I do not think about it much, but I know if I wanted to, I could still pull up those images mentally and "see" them.

That First Experience

It is kind of crazy, but even though my initial experience with pornography was over forty years ago, I can still remember feeling a multitude of emotional responses as we flipped through the pages of that magazine. I felt a bunch of things at once…excitement, awkwardness, shame, and fear.

I guess the reason I felt excitement because the experience was strange and new. Never had I seen anything like this before! And though it was a mystery (I had no clue what I was looking at), it still intrigued me and drew me in. I wanted to see more. Why didn't they have any clothes on? Why were these people standing or lying like that? What was on the next page? All these physical images of things happening between a boy and a girl I had never seen before. So many questions that my mind was unable to provide me with answers to. Like I said, I had no clue, but I wanted to see more!

There was awkwardness as well. The whole situation felt weird. I am not sure why, but it that felt like I should not be looking at this stuff with my friend and his brother and sister there. Their presence felt wrong, like maybe I should be alone...or at least just me and my friend. I did not know his brother or sister very well, but for some reason my young mind reasoned they should not be there.

The main emotion I can remember experiencing is that I felt ashamed. Shame because there was some level of understanding in me that people were not supposed to be taking their clothes off in front of other people, especially in front of girls! And yet there they were, both girls and boys naked with each other! And we were looking at them! Of course, they were not really there, but there they were...right in front of us. And I was looking at them without their clothes on. I do not know if I felt ashamed because I was looking at them naked like that or if I felt ashamed for them because they were naked in front of me, but I was ashamed anyway.

And boy was there fear! Fear of being caught. Because somehow, in some way, I felt this was wrong and that our parents might find out! What would they say about this if they knew? What would they do to me? How long would I be grounded for? Would I get the belt? Would I never be able to play with my friend again? Who knew? I just knew I did not want my parents to know...or anyone else for that matter!

To be honest, I think I was too young to be physically aroused by the images that flipped before my eyes as my buddy turned the pages. A boy of ten does not always begin the process of puberty that early in life. However, I definitely knew this had to do with a topic I had heard whispered in discussions I wasn't supposed to be a part of. This had to do with the "S" word—S-E-X. A word I would only spell out before, never say out loud. This was part of the world I had yet to be included in. But not anymore! Now I had a secret invitation to start thinking about sex and a new passage into that world. In the days to come, I would often revisit those images in my mind.

The amount of time we spent looking at that magazine probably amounted to about ten minutes, but it was enough to give my appetite a taste for fruit I had been forbidden to taste before. And deep down I liked it. I was not too sure why, but I did.

A few days later at school, I found out that my friend was confronted by his parents about his little discovery. And though I did not ask him, I am fairly certain his little sister told on him. But I for sure did ask him if he got in trouble! He said, "No. My dad just told me that what I saw in that book wasn't what sex was like and that when I was older, he would explain it to me." That was the extent of their discussion about the situation…and ours too for that matter. And though we never spoke of it again, I thought about it regularly. I never told anyone else about it, and as far as I know, they never told my parents. At least they never talked with me about it.

In retrospect, as I think about that question of whether they told my parents, there is the possibility that they could have let them know but that they did not really want to breach that subject with me. Not too long after this experience that I discovered I did not have to wait to find a magazine thrown out in a pile of rubbish to have access to pornography. It was closer to home than I would have ever guessed. Maybe the reason Dad did not feel like he could tell me that I should not look at pornography was because he did.

Everybody Does It

I do not remember the first time I discovered pornography was in our home, but I know it was shortly after this experience at my friend's house. Whether I came across it as I dug through my parents' dresser or hiding in their closet or if it was found buried under the linens in the bathroom, I did eventually come across it. In time, I found every place my father had chosen to hide it. In no time at all I was viewing my dad's pornography regularly. And even though it was difficult for me to be alone growing up in a house with eight other siblings, that just required me to get creative. Mostly this meant my time going to the bathroom or taking showers took much longer than necessary!

You can be sure that the presence of pornography in my own home communicated some things to me. The first thing it told me was that it was normal. I realize I had not seen it before and that pornography was not out in the open for all to see, but the reality that it was here in our home solidified the concept that magazines with naked people in them was not that strange. I assumed my dad was normal. Every kid does. If my dad had pornography, then it stood to reason that dads just had it. That must be the way it is. Why would anybody else's dad be different than mine?

Another thing porn in my home communicated to me was that it is definitely meant to be hidden. Every single piece of pornography I ever came across in our home was hidden. Whether it was a magazine or a book or a video, I noticed they were all out of sight where people would not be able to find them. I thought I must have been lucky or clever to have found my dad's stash, but I could see very clearly that they had been buried in order to keep others out. And whenever I wanted to get into it, I tried to make sure I would put them back exactly as I found them. I reasoned that if I put it back in the wrong drawer or upside down or out of order, then someone would know I had been there. Memorizing the precise location a magazine or video was in before I got there ensured that no one would know I had been messing with their valuables. It would all go unnoticed…hidden and out of sight.

One more thing I "learned" about porn from it being in our home was that I got to use it. Finding it under my own roof kind of gave me an unofficial "permission" to look at it whenever I could. If I could be clever enough about how and when, and if I kept it a secret, I could get into these treasures and indulge as much as I wanted. Keeping it hidden and secret, just like Dad had, was the key to me maintaining my privilege of viewing pornography.

One thing is for sure for me, once I discovered my dad's pornography, it became a regular part of growing up. I did not give any thought to how pornography was influencing my developing perspective about sex. I did not contemplate the spiritual dynamics of giving the devil an opportunity to pervert my heart. That entire time, the devil used pornography (and other things) to turn sex into an idol in my life. I was over my head in the deep end of the pool without a life preserver…and I did not know how to swim. Thoughts were being influenced and developed in my head concerning sex, and pornography was the teacher.

What's the Matter with a Little Porn?

Pornography has become a rampant problem in our society. What once stood on trial in our judicial system as being a vulgar criminal activity[4] has been turned into a multibillion-dollar industry which exploits the lives of millions of people. The internet has contributed to the widespread use of pornography by people from all walks of life. Adults, children, male, female, religious, rich, poor…no segment of society is immune to falling prey to its lure. Thirty-five percent of all data transferred across the internet is pornographic. At any given second of the day there are over 28,000 people viewing porn online. Not per day, not an hour, not at any given minute of the day…every second! And every second of the day the porn industry takes in over $3,000. The increase of violence in pornography has continued to rise so that now, 88 percent of all scenes contain some form of physical aggression. Marriages continue to be negatively impacted by porn to the point that near six out of every ten divorces involved one of the spouses being obsessed with online pornographic websites. Acceptance of pornography in our society is now the new norm to the point where most teenagers believe that not recycling is a worse offense than using pornography.[5]

Many men have used pornography so frequently that it has become a stronghold in their lives or a bondage they feel they will never be free from. Sexual addiction disorders, erectile dysfunction, counseling men struggling with overcoming pornography…these things are all on the rise in our society. Solomon warned us,

> Hell and destruction are never full. So the eyes of men are never satisfied. (Proverbs 27:20 NKJV)

The use of porn will only lead to more use of it. Men cannot get enough to ever be satisfied by viewing pornography. Studies have

---

4   Larry Flynt (publisher of Hustler pornographic magazine) was brought to court multiple times for violating obscenity laws.
5   Enough.org, CovenantEyes.com.

shown that the more a man uses pornography, the more difficulty they will have performing physically in bed. They are forced to envision pornographic images in order to maintain an erection during sexual intercourse.[6] This is a drastically different concept than what we may have thought about using pornography!

In spite of the statistical proofs that porn is a major issue, most people do not see any problem with using pornography. The world presents it as an acceptable means of learning about sex. Or they see it as a means of sexual fulfillment for someone who is not being fulfilled elsewhere. A counselor or psychologist might encourage others to use it, just so long as it is done in moderation. Many men justify their use of pornography, maybe not openly, but in their minds, and they have reasoned that pornography is not that bad. Some are even convinced that it is helpful! They do not see anything wrong with looking a little here or there.

Though others would not decry the negatives of porn, there is no doubt about it: pornography is a serious issue plaguing our society these days. The sad reality is that secular society is not the only victim of porn. The perversions and sinful lusts of pornography have infiltrated the church and continue to infect the mind of many Christian men today. This reality must be addressed!

Though our society may allow for the use of pornography, the biblical perspective is that a mentality which justifies it is a worldly approach to a sinful activity. The Bible does not agree with such reasoning and as a Christian man, neither should you. Notice what the apostle Paul says in Ephesians 5:6–17 NIV:

> Let no one deceive you with empty words, for because of such things God's wrath comes on those who are disobedient. Therefore do not be partners with them. For you were once darkness, but now you are light in the Lord. Live as children of the light (for the fruit of the light consists in all goodness, righteousness and truth) and find out

---

6   WebMD.com, "Study see link between Porn and Sexual Dysfunction."

what pleases the Lord. Have nothing to do with the fruitless deeds of darkness, but rather expose them. It is shameful even to mention what the disobedient do in secret. But everything exposed by the light becomes visible—and everything that is illuminated becomes a light. That is why it is said: "Wake up, sleeper, rise from the dead, and Christ will shine on you." Be very careful, then, how you live—not as unwise but as wise, making the most of every opportunity, because the days are evil. Therefore do not be foolish, but understand what the Lord's will is.

When it comes to worldly perspectives, the admonition is that Christians are not to partner with those that promote or adhere to them. They live in darkness, but we are light in the Lord. We are called to have nothing to do with their approach to things, especially a sinful thing like pornography. When men are disobedient to the instructions of God, their "alone times" (what they do in secret) become opportunities to engage in shameful behavior. Sexual idolatry lulls men into a sleep which Jesus is calling us to wake up from. And when it comes to pornography, we are not to be so foolish as to think there is nothing wrong with it, even with just a little.

If you think about it, the dynamic present in the use of pornography should automatically let you know that there is something wrong with it. Not many men use pornography openly.[7] It is almost always used privately and in secret. The normal emotional response for a man when he uses pornography is shame. Sometimes he will even promise himself he will not do it again. And if someone walks in on them! The situation quickly turns into a no-holds-barred effort to hide what they are doing. Buttons on the remote get pushed, laptops get slammed down, hands go up in front of the screen...every

---

[7] I have met very few men who are openly proud of the fact that they use pornography. Those that I have met are usually men who have seared their conscience over time by ignoring and suppressing the feelings of guilt and shame as they continually engage in sinful behavior.

attempt is made to hide so others will not see what they were just looking at.

Embarrassment and shame are the common emotional experience for men who use pornography. And I should encourage you that this is a good thing! Those feelings of shame are our God-given conscience telling us that something is wrong with our behavior. The fact that we feel the need to hide our use of pornography, and the guilt and shame we feel when we do, should be clear indicators to us that the activity is wrong to begin with!

But there is so much more that is sinful associated with pornography than just our need to hide and our sense of shame. Everything involved with pornography is condemned in the Bible. Fornication, adultery, voyeurism, nudity, lust, perversions of normal sexual activity, rape, incest, homosexuality, even bestiality…those who produce pornography seem to intentionally go to the extreme in rebelling against every restriction God has given us concerning human sexuality. They have perverted what is good in every way possible. As Paul said in the verse above, "because of such things God's wrath comes on those who are disobedient." Christian men must not partner with those who rebel against God and pervert what is holy and good.

However, beyond the obvious sinful elements present in pornography (and there are many), there are hidden poisons included as well. Men who engage in regular use of pornography have allowed it to create unhealthy and unrealistic expectations of sex. Men who have been taught by porn what sex is supposed to be like bring a distorted concept of sex to their marriage bed. This distortion prevents them from experiencing sex in marriage as God intended. Minds perverted by pornography have developed a system of thought which creates a never-ending cycle of failure. They feel like their sex life has failed them. The sex they experience in their marriage bed does not deliver on a promise pornography made to them! And it is all because their view of sex has been distorted.

What might some of those distortions be? There could be a lot of them! Here are a few to consider…

Maybe as men "taught" by pornography they expect sex to be easy and often. They may have elevated the importance of sex to the degree that they think it is the most important thing in their marriage. They might expect their wives to be like women in the fantasy world pornography created in their minds. Distortions are not only limited to those things, but very often men who have been influenced by pornography have connected who they are as a man to how well they perform in bed. The devil has set them up by getting them to believe that what happens in the fantasy world of pornography is what they should expect in their own bedroom. And then, when sex in real life is not like sex in pornography, the disappointment hits hard. Expectations fall short and difficulties rise. Their use of pornography has turned the wonder of sex with their own wife into a second-rate experience that left them feeling cheated. The enemy of our marriages loves it when our sexual encounters are major disappointments.

But wait…there's more!

The problems with pornography are multifaceted. It is like a virus that reproduces itself… Pornography is a disease with many symptoms!

I once heard a pastor do a message on pornography, and one of the points he made has really stuck with me. He declared emphatically, "The problem with pornography is that there is not enough sex in it!" Most of the audience internally responded by saying to themselves, "How can that be? Pornography is nothing but sex!" That internal response reveals exactly what he was trying to communicate. Men think of sex as merely physical. His point was that God intended sex to be more than just an activity that happens with our bodies. There is so much more that goes into a husband and wife experiencing good sex than what happens under the sheets. A smile from across the room that lets her know you like her, asking how her day went when you get home, helping clean off the table after supper, working together in the yard, holding her hand at the restaurant, doing devotions and praying together, communication, patience, forgiveness—you know, all the things that good marriages need! His point was that pornography does not include the numerous loving interactions outside of our bedrooms that contribute to a husband and wife enjoying true physical intimacy inside our bedrooms! There is more to good sex than just a mere physical interaction! God designed sex to be good when a husband and wife connect on emotional and intellectual and spiritual levels that lead to truly connecting on a physical level. There is so much more to sex than meets the eye. Pornography leaves all that out!

And finally let me just point out that pornography is a selfish thing. The use of pornography is entirely focused on pleasing ourselves. Jesus specifically told us that if we want to be His followers, we must deny ourselves, take up our cross, and follow Him. Not only is behavior that is self-pleasing specifically against what it means to be a disciple of Jesus Christ; being focused on pleasing yourself is not what sex was intended to be. Sex was created by God to be a *mutually* fulfilling activity between a man and his wife, where a married couple both gives and receives pleasure to the person they have lovingly committed to be with the rest of their lives. The use of pornography eliminates the giving and receiving pleasure from another and puts all the emphasis on pleasing yourself.

Conclusion

The Christian who has had any level of interaction with pornography must begin to deal with it biblically. In saying that I mean to communicate that we have to think and act in line with what the Bible teaches us and apply it to our perspective about porn. If it is a part of your past, recognize the potential damage it has done and seek the help of God for healing that damage. Root out any mentality which may remain in your current thoughts about sex which pornography has "taught" you. If it is a part of your life now, do the hard work of repentance and replacement that growing and changing as a believer in Christ requires of you (which we will discuss more in later chapters).

We cannot play games with pornography, even in our thoughts. How we approach it must honor God by staying true to His Word.

King David said, "I will place no wicked thing before my eyes." Job declared, "I have made a covenant with my eyes not to look upon a maiden." Jesus taught us, "If a man looks upon a woman lustfully, he has committed adultery in his heart." Paul taught the Thessalonian church that there should not even be the hint of sexual immorality among them. In almost every list of sins found in the New Testament we are told to remove from our lives, sexual immorality is at the top of the list, and whether the world wants to admit it or not, *pornography is sexually immoral.* The church of Jesus Christ has extremely clear instructions pertaining to holy and pure living which would remove and keep any element of sexual impurity from our lives. If you are a part of that church, then pornography should get the right foot of fellowship and get kicked out of every aspect of who you are!

CHAPTER 3

SEXUAL IDOLS ON DISPLAY

> Son of man, these men have set up idols in their
> hearts and put wicked stumbling blocks before their
> faces. Should I let them inquire of me at all?
> —Ezekiel 14:3 NIV

One of the realities of human dynamic is that what is on the inside rises to the surface. The things of the heart eventually manifest themselves externally. That which resides in thought and desire display themselves in speech and behavior. When sex has become an idol in the heart of a man it begins to make itself known in our lives. The idol gets put up "on a shelf." Idolatry always manifests itself.

Jesus spoke of this reality in many places. He taught us that it is from the overflow of the heart that the mouth speaks. He said you could know a tree, whether it had good roots or not, by its fruit. And He spoke of the defiling factor of the heart displaying itself in external behaviors in Mark 7:20–23 NKJV:

> What comes out of a man, that defiles a
> man. For from within, out of the heart of men,
> proceed evil thoughts, adulteries, fornications,
> murders, thefts, covetousness, wickedness, deceit,
> lewdness, an evil eye, blasphemy, pride, foolish-

ness. All these evil things come from within and defile a man.

Notice the emphasis on the heart producing external manifestations of sin. "All these evil things come from within." Like a pregnant woman, the baby growing on the inside begins to physically show itself and eventually comes out, the presence of an idol in our hearts creates the sure result that we will give birth to sin in our lives. I am purposefully stealing the "pregnant" imagery from James when I speak of giving birth to sin in our lives. Listen to how James puts it:

> Each one is tempted when he is drawn away by his own desires and enticed. Then, when desire has conceived, it gives birth to sin; and sin, when it is full-grown, brings forth death. (James 1:14–15 NKJV)

Desires conceived in the heart grow until they eventually give birth to sin. This is a spiritual truth which cannot be resisted or denied… An idol present in our hearts cannot help but manifest sinfully in our behavior. It is a good idea to put our desire to the test to see we have made an idol of it. Remember this idolatry test from chapter 1? One of the best litmus tests for idolatry is found in the answer to these questions:

Am I willing to sin in order to get my desire fulfilled?

Do I sin as a result of not having my desire fulfilled?

Do I run to this thing when I am looking for a refuge?

I do not know who developed this three-question litmus test, but it has been extremely helpful to determine if I have exalted *any* desire to the point of making it into an idol. I intend to unpack this litmus test later in the book, but I wanted to mention them here to highlight a certain reality. The presence of sin associated with the self-focused fulfillment of a specific desire can reveal idolatry. In other words, when sex becomes an idol in our hearts, we can be sure it will reveal itself in sinful ways. Let's explore the possible external manifestations of sexual idolatry hidden in the heart of a man.

Masturbation

The first point of discussion has to do with the "need" to fulfill yourself sexually. Different segments of our culture have described this activity in various ways ranging from very vulgar to extremely silly, but the technical term for what we are talking about is masturbation. This is the process of stimulating yourself sexually. Masturbation is usually intended to result in ejaculation but does not need to end that way in order to be considered masturbation. Any level of self-inflicted sexual stimulation can be considered masturbation.

In the Christian community there are debates over whether Christians should condemn masturbation as a sinful behavior or simply allow it a pass, seeing it as a natural, or even healthy expression of human sexuality. Some allow for it with the impression that the Bible does not say anything about it and conclude that because of biblical silence on the matter, we should not include additional, unnecessary prohibitions pertaining to sexual expression. I am obviously wading into this discussion and so I will throw in my two cents on the matter by challenging that observation... Is the Bible silent on the topic of masturbation? I do not think so.

There are a few places where we could look for the topic to be addressed, but I am only going to highlight one. This is a passage found in the Sermon on the Mount where Jesus is expounding on the commandment against adultery. Listen to how Jesus expects us to apply the command against adultery:

> You have heard that it was said to those of old, "You shall not commit adultery." But I say to you that whoever looks at a woman to lust for her has already committed adultery with her in his heart. If your right eye causes you to sin, pluck it out and cast it from you; for it is more profitable for you that one of your members perish, than for your whole body to be cast into hell. And if your right hand causes you to sin, cut it off and cast it from you; for it is more profitable for you

that one of your members perish, than for your
whole body to be cast into hell. (Matthew 5:27–
30 NKJV)

It seems fairly obvious to all listening that Jesus expects us to
see that there is more involved in the command against adultery than
just cheating on your wife. His intent is to get to the heart of the
matter which would give birth to the act of adultery. He is aiming
His crosshairs at the presence of lust in a man's heart. Lust in the
heart is defined as breaking the commandment against adultery. "He
has already committed adultery with her in his heart." Pretty clear
condemnation of lustful thoughts, I would say. However, Jesus has
more to say about the matter and continues by pointing out the connection of sexual sin with the eyes and the hands. If your right eye
causes you to sin, cut it off. If your right hand causes you to sin, cut
it off. The extreme approach to sinful expression in the sexual department is applied to the eye and the hand. In my mind, this is a pretty
clear description of masturbation.

But the bigger application is the more important one. People
could get very creative in masturbating without violating the instructions here. They could masturbate without looking at or creating a
mental picture of a woman when they do. They could find a way to
masturbate without using their right hand (perhaps the left one works
almost as well) or they could accomplish the feat without using their
hands at all. But this would only indicate exactly what Jesus was getting at in explaining the commandment against adultery. It is not the
literal exactitude of the command that God has in mind but rather
where a man's heart is concerning sex. Why are we contemplating the
act of masturbation? Why do we feel it necessary? What is driving a
man to think they "need" to pleasure themselves?

There can be many answers to those questions I am sure. God
is concerned with the motive driving the act. Can you say without a
doubt that when you masturbate there is no sinful intention or perversion of God's design for sex? Is there the absence of lust? Is there
the absence of sensuality? Is there a pure desire to honor God in the
way we deal with our sexual desires and urges? These are important

elements in determining whether something is appropriate sexually for us!

I deliberately used the word "urges" in the last paragraph as a segue to introduce the next verse I want to bring up. Men frequently refer to their sexual desires as urges. The reference to sex as an urge may be meant to communicate that their sexual desires are natural and strong. But I think there is also intent to communicate that these desires are also meant to be fulfilled, should not be resisted, or, even worse, that we cannot help but do something to fulfill these urges. The notion is promoted that the sexual urge present in us comes from our bodies. Our hormones are flowing through our bloodstream expecting the desires they create to be met. Physically speaking we are being driven by urges that propel us to act upon them. I mean, why else would we have an erection if it is not meant to result in us seeking physical release from it? This is a mind-set which men deal with which cannot be ignored and therefore should not be ignored!

Listen to me close, Christian man: the idea that you are merely a physical being driven by biological forces is not a biblical reality, and sexual release is not a "need" you must have met. If anyone wants to argue for engaging in masturbation as appropriate behavior on account of it being a biological experience, then I would answer by saying it is just as much of a biological truth that a man will not die if he does not have sex or experience sexual release. Meaning, that if you experience an erection, it does not mean that you absolutely must also experience ejaculation as a result.

Here is the thing we all need to know as Christian men: you are not only made up of flesh and bones and hormones and urges. The Bible acknowledges very clearly that we are physical beings that must contend with ourselves and our biological situations. But it also promotes the idea that we are more than just physical. We are spiritual as well. And as such *we are not to be controlled by our bodies but rather control them* in a way that honors God. Notice what Paul says to the Thessalonian church in 1 Thessalonians 4:3–5 NIV:

> It is God's will that you should be sanctified: that you should avoid sexual immorality;

that each of you should learn to control your own
body in a way that is holy and honorable, not in
passionate lust like the pagans, who do not know
God.

You have a body, no doubt about it. If you are a man who has
gone through puberty, you also have hormones that course through
your body which create sexual urges, no denying that. But God presents us with the reality that those sexual urges can be *controlled* in
a way that is holy and honorable. It is something that we can learn
to do, and according to this verse, learning to do so is a part of our
sanctification—our growing and maturing to be more like Christ. As
Christians, we do not allow our biological urges to control us, but
rather the ultimate controlling factor in our lives is to be our desire
to please God.

I need to highlight one more aspect of this verse before moving
on. Notice how Paul differentiates between God's men who know
him and the pagans who do not? He is intending to communicate
that to live our lives from the perspective that our body controls us
instead of the other way around is a pagan approach to life. The
thought "We are only human and can't help ourselves" is not a
Christian mind-set. They (pagans) live lives based on what their biological desires dictate. We are to live life based on what pleases and
glorifies God!

Fornication: Sex Before Marriage

Our culture teaches us to frown on the concept of virginity.
The idea that a man would save himself for marriage has become
an object of ridicule or a sign that a man is not a man. Young men
in high school help promote the notion "You ain't nothing if you
haven't had sex." If you had not had sex by high school, something
is wrong with you. When I was in school, the accusation was that
you were gay. That might not fly these days, but the dynamic is still
the same. Peers push one another to engage in more and more sexual
activity as a proof that you are someone. You are a man.

I have found myself in many different men's ministry situations and in some of them I have presented to the group the question of when a man first becomes a man, or when they first felt like they were a man. There are a number of different responses to this question, like, "My first job" or "When I got my driver's license." Some men have even said, "When I got married." But the most popular response is almost always "The first time I had sex." That is interesting to consider...the notion that someone could not feel like or consider themselves to be a man until they had sex. There is something fundamentally wrong with a society that has this perspective as an underlying, foundational understanding of manhood—that a young man could not think of himself as a man until he has had sex with a girl.

The popular view about sex among the youth of our culture is idolatrous. They have placed a high value on those who engage in sexual activity. Being cool or being someone who they can look up to all too often includes this sinful notion. The more our culture drifts away from God, the more we should expect this reality; it is a foolish notion to expect anything else. The problem I am more interested in addressing is the way these perspectives invade the Christian community. Our young men are being increasingly influenced by worldly idols. Their peers, even their Christian peers, accept and promote a secular conception concerning their developing ideas about sex.

And young people are not the only ones promoting sex before marriage. Almost every educator who runs our sex ed classes encourages the next generation to enjoy sexual activity with their partner, just so long as they are practicing safe sex. The reasoning is "They are going to do it anyway. They might as well be protected from sexually transmitted diseases or unwanted pregnancies." Any effort to discourage or eliminate those voices from speaking to our youth are quickly silenced and often branded as old-fashioned, Victorian sticks in the mud whose main purpose in life is to rob others of happiness or pleasure. Like Paul said to the Thessalonians, "like the pagans, who do not know God."

I am sorry to report this same dynamic is present in our churches as well. It is not uncommon among youth ministries, youth groups, and youth events that the biblical view about sexuality is set aside and replaced with what the world promotes. A sad reality is that sexual activity is engaged in during youth groups and youth events regularly. Compromise of standards by youth pastors, many of whom are struggling with an idolatrous perspective of sexuality themselves, is often communicated to the young "sheep" they are called to pastor.

While researching pornography use among Christians, it was shocking for me when I came across the statistics on porn use among youth leaders and youth pastors. Almost 70 percent of youth pastors struggle with their own pornography use![8] When that is the reality in private, it will manifest in external way, and very often it will manifest itself in discussions, advice, and counsel. Obviously, this is not true across the board for every youth worker or pastor out there, but this reality is entirely too frequent in Christian circles as that seven out of ten statistic confirms. As young men get older, the situation just continues down a wrong road.

Living together before getting married makes sense to a sensual society. "Gotta test-drive the car before you buy it!" is the normal proverbial explanation for premarital sex, right? The words themselves betray they think of sex as an idol, don't they? It's as if they are saying, "I can't have a wife who isn't everything I want in the bedroom, and so I have to find out if our sex life will be what I expect before I walk the aisle. If she does not measure up to what my idol tells me sex should be like, I will have a terrible marriage." In the real world, the quality of marriage is built on much more than just sex, but a heart that has turned sex into an idol cannot see it any other way. They cannot imagine a good, God-honoring marriage that does not include what their idolatrous hearts have imagined sex to be.

Fornication has infected the minds of our young adults. We have been in the midst of a pretty disturbing trend in our culture lately: the acceptance of the notion that marriage is becoming obsolete! In 2010, researchers surveyed eighteen to twenty-nine-year-olds and discovered that nearly half (44%) thought marriage was not

---

[8] Enough.org, "Christians and Online Porn."

important![9] The number of couples cohabitating ("shacking up," as we used to call it) is consistently rising in our country while the number of married couples dwindles. Fornication is not only limited to cohabitating couples sleeping together before they are married either. Casual sex has become a regular part of accepted behavior: hooking up, friends with benefits, one-night stands, sexting, sexperiments, etc.... We have grown into a society that has effectively removed many of the cultural boundaries prohibiting sex before marriage.

I want to revisit the verse in 1 Thessalonians we looked at in the previous section because I stopped short of the entire passage concerning our sexual sanctification which Paul was speaking of there. Let's see the passage in its entirety.

> It is God's will that you should be sanctified: that you should avoid sexual immorality; that each of you should learn to control your own body in a way that is holy and honorable, not in passionate lust like the pagans, who do not know God; and that in this matter no one should wrong or take advantage of a brother or sister. The Lord will punish all those who commit such sins, as we told you and warned you before. For God did not call us to be impure, but to live a holy life. Therefore, anyone who rejects this instruction does not reject a human being but God, the very God who gives you his Holy Spirit. (1 Thessalonians 4:3–8 NIV)

Fornication wrongs our brothers and sisters. When we sleep with a woman who is not our wife, we sin against her. We have received from her something we should only experience if we have willingly committed ourselves to a lifelong covenant of companionship. We have taken from her that which was not ours to take. When we sleep with a woman who is not our wife, we have robbed her future hus-

---

[9] Statistica.com, "Do You Agree That Marriage Is Becoming Obsolete?"

band of the blessing God intended their marriage to experience. It is only her husband who is rightfully allowed by God to share that level of intimacy with. When we sleep with a woman who is not our wife, we rob our future wife of the blessing God intended sex to bring to our marriage. The pursual of sex prior to marriage is a sinful expression of the idol in our heart.

The marriage bed was always intended by God to be pure, unpolluted by sexual sin. If we do not come into our marriages as virgins, we have set the stage for the marriage bed to be polluted, polluting it before we have even "made the bed," so to speak. "God did not call us to be impure, but to live a holy life." Painting those who are against sex before marriage as people who are out to rob you of pleasure and keep you from having fun is just plain wrong. It is not "joy robbing" humans who have instituted such a "strict" approach to sex before marriage; it was God. Fornication is a flat-out rejection of God and His intention for sex.

The idolization of sex continues to move our society further and further from God's intent for it, and fornication is just one of the ways this idol has manifest itself.

Adultery

An obvious expression of sexual idolatry is the sin of adultery. Defining adultery is not difficult: adultery is when a married individual has a sexual experience with someone other than their spouse. This sinful behavior is expressly forbidden in the Scriptures in multiple places and with strong words. The inclusion of adultery as one of the Ten Commandments is good evidence that God expects us to take it seriously. As we read through the New Testament, we also find the same level of seriousness given to the topic. Every list of sins we are instructed to put to death or remove from our lives usually has adultery or fornication at the top of the list. God is very serious about purity in sexual expression and that it is to be limited to the confines of marriage. Even a casual reader of the Bible knows this to be true. For that matter, even most people who do not read the Bible knows this to be true!

We can almost say without exception that every marriage ceremony these days includes a public confession, charge, and promise to not commit adultery. "Forsaking all others..." (or some other form of lifelong commitment) is spoken with the express purpose of communicating we will be sexually faithful and committed to our wives "until death, do we part." I do not doubt that most husbands standing at the altar or in front of the judge mean to be true to those words. Of course, there are exceptions to that last statement as some husbands may have even been unfaithful in that department the night before at their bachelor party. But overall, I believe most husbands mean to keep the promise of sexual faithfulness made in their vow.

So what is it that causes a man to break that vow and commit adultery?

I admit that the answer to that question can be multifaceted. People are a complicated mess of different thoughts and experiences that combine to make us who we are. However, I would like to propose that sexual idolatry is at least one of the main ingredients which contributes to husbands breaking their vows of sexual faithfulness. The fashioning of sex into an idol in the hearts of men creates the fertile ground for adultery to occur.

Remember our verse from James 1? Desire conceived in the heart grows and matures until it gives birth to sin. Wrong thoughts and desires in our hearts are constantly moving us toward outward expressions of sinful behavior. This is no less true when it comes to adultery. When we turn sex into an idol, it will display itself somehow. All idols require us to worship and serve them. We will serve and worship what we idolize. An idol is never content to simply stay hidden in our hearts but will display itself in our lives. The outward expression of sin comes after we have done the inner work of fashioning the idol into the image we desire. Over time our hearts carve and form our thoughts, opinions, and desires concerning sex, almost without notice, until one day what is inside comes out.

I remember listening to a counselor recount an experience he had with someone he was counseling with on account of them cheating on their wife. The man maintained that his adultery occurred suddenly and without plan or intent on his part. The counselor tried without success to convince the man otherwise and was getting a little frustrated with the situation. The counselor then adopted an ingenious approach to communicate his point. On the desk in front of him was a stack of books and papers. As they continued to speak, every couple of seconds he would reach over and push the pile a little closer to the edge of the desk. Eventually the pile was teetering on the edge, ready to fall off. A little later and the counselor reached over and gave one last little shove and the pile crashed onto the floor. "How on earth did that happen?" he asked the counselee, doing his best to pretend to be surprised. "You pushed it off the table... What did you expect?" was his response. "But I only pushed it once."

"No, you didn't..." the man paused mid-sentence as the realization finally occurred to him. We do not jump right into big sins all at once; we move toward them slowly and methodically in our hearts and minds.

The pile of books did not get from the middle of the desk to the office floor in one quick push but little by little. Although adultery occurs in a moment of time, we get there little by little in our thoughts and desires. I think it was John MacArthur that once said, "When a man falls into sexual sin he doesn't fall far." He has moved there slowly, to the edge of the desk so to speak, in his heart.

A man comes to cheat on his wife through many little thoughts and desires which occur in his heart concerning sex. For instance, if pornography has been the tool which carved out our image about sex, we have developed expectations of what fulfilling sex is supposed to be like. Let me flesh out what I mean with a few questions to highlight what ideas we might develop on account of pornography:

- How often should a husband and wife have sex? Does pornography answer that question? Does it communicate anything to us about how often we should engage in sex in order for our "sex life" to be fulfilling and wonderful? Of course it does! Sex all the time! Sex every chance you get! Sex is all people ever think about! Those are the things we pick up on from pornography. When our sex life is not that way, we begin to think something is wrong.

- How about this question... How long should sex last? Can a man or a woman enjoy sex if it is over quickly? Pornography teaches that sex should last long and incorporate as much possible variety in one experience. Is that the way sex always is, or can it be short in duration and still be fulfilling? What have we come to think about concerning the length of time our sexual encounters should measure up to? The expectations we have developed can quickly turn into disappointments if we have allowed pornography to answer these questions for us.

- Here is another good question to consider: How should my wife respond if I am pleasing her? How should she "act" if she is enjoying sex?[10] One of the things I have come to realize in talking with other men who struggle with sexual issues (as well as from my own struggles in this department) is that husbands are most fulfilled sexually if they know their wife is fulfilled sexually. They just want their wife to enjoy making love to them. Pornography tells men how women "act" when they enjoy sex and we want that experience. When our wives do not act like the women in the movies, we can conclude that our wives do not enjoy sex with us, and we are not pleasing them. This is unfair to our wives, but it is often something many of them contend with.

These are just a few questions to consider... The list could go on and on, but I hope you can recognize the point I am trying to make. Pornography told us things and we believe them, and even though pornography is not the only place where we get our images from, it highlights the reality well. We fashion an idea in our heads

---

[10] I use the word "act" here purposefully to remind men that women in pornography are paid performers. They are putting on a show. Expecting similar "performances" from your wife is not what God intended sexual intimacy to be like. Thankfully, your wife is not the woman on the screen.

about what our sexual experience with our wife ought to be like and bring those expectations to our bedrooms. When those expectations fall short, we may feel cheated. We may feel rejected. We may feel inadequate. We may feel our wife is inadequate. We may conclude that our sexual experiences are inadequate.

Husbands that cheat on their wives are neither thankful nor content. They feel like they are missing out on something. Something better. Something more. More fulfilling. More pleasing. More satisfying. Something more in line with the image they have fashioned in their heart. Adultery is a chance to worship and serve their idol.

Perversions

Turning sex into an idol can lead men down some pretty dark roads. Beyond the list of ways this idol displays itself which I have already addressed, there are many more. Some of those manifestations are pretty shameful to address or admit to. Mankind seems to have a propensity for creativity when it comes to perverting what is good and right and holy. Rape, incest, homosexuality, sexual abuse, child pornography, bestiality, sadism, and masochism—these sinful manifestations are just the beginning of a long list of ways men can and have twisted God's good gift of sex. Our idols require more and more from us in the ways we serve them, searching continually for the satisfaction they promise but never give. Perversions of sex can lead us to display some pretty disgusting expressions of human behavior. It is what idolatry does to us. And when sex becomes an idol in our hearts, we should beware of how far down that road it could lead us.

Wrapping it up...

This chapter has been pretty discouraging to write. Talking about sin, addressing sin, exposing sin...it is never a fun or comfortable thing for me. However, one thing I have learned is that we do not overcome sin or find freedom from it if it is not addressed. Sweeping sin under the rug only complicates our lives and circumstances. "Whoever conceals their sins does not prosper..." (Proverbs 28:13a NIV). When God confronts sin, He does so with the end goal in mind: to "forgive us our sins and cleanse us from all unrighteousness" (1 John 1:9b NKJV).

Ultimately sin will be judged and condemned. The theme verse for this book communicates that very definitely:

> Marriage should be honored by all, and the marriage bed kept pure, for God will judge the adulterer and all the sexually immoral. (Hebrews 13:4 NIV)

God will judge sexual idolatry and sexual sin. Sometimes that judgment comes in the form of reaping what we have sown. The disappointments and frustrations we have experienced in our bedrooms are a good example of that. But a bigger judgment is also coming: the Day of Judgment. That is a guarantee which the Bible promises. But until that day comes, God wants to redeem us from the seeds our sinful natures have planted in our lives. He desires that we would be set free from sin. He longs to forgive and lead us out of sin and into the liberty He has designed for us. He desires that our marriage beds be pure, free from our sinful ideas about what sex should be. God wants us to enjoy sex in our marriages, but He knows it will never be all He wanted it to be for us as long as we idolize it. He is aware of how sexual sins kill the intimacy He intended to be present in our marriage beds. He knows how the flesh destroys the purpose He created sex for. He knows that our idolatry robs our marriage of the blessing sex is supposed to bring. It angers Him when men pervert what He has intended to be pure and good. And it grieves Him when marriages are missing this blessed piece of the puzzle.

Thank God that even though He is the Judge of sin, He is also a merciful and forgiving God who wants to forgive our sins. He can redeem our pasts and transform our futures. Though the consequences of sexual idolatry might continue to impact our present-day circumstances, the more we walk in line with the truths of God's Word and the perfection of His will we can experience the healing and grace associated with His love.

Forgiveness, mercy, freedom…these manifestations of God's grace are inherently linked to the biblical injunction for us to repent and turn from our sinful ways. Repentance recognizes the gravity of our sin. Repentance communicates that we realize an idol in our hearts has perverted the goodness of God's blessings in exchange for our own selfish and fleshly desires. Repentance owns responsibility for the presence of an idol in our hearts and the way we have allowed that idol to express itself in our actions. Repentance admits that sexual immorality is wicked. And repentance turns from it completely, not only in our actions but also our minds and thoughts. Repentance puts us in line with God's good plans for what sex is supposed to be. And finally, repentance begins to purify our marriage beds because it seeks to remove from our lives those things that would defile it.

In a couple of chapters, we are going to look pretty intently into how we are called to destroy the idols in our lives and the steps we can take to rid our hearts of sexual idolatry. However, before we go there, I want to first spend some time highlighting the damage that making an idol out of sex can create in our lives and in our marriages.

CHAPTER 4

DAMAGE REPORT

Do not be deceived: God cannot be mocked. A man
reaps what he sows. Whoever sows to please their flesh,
from the flesh will reap destruction; whoever sows to
please the Spirit, from the Spirit will reap eternal life.
—Galatians 6:7–8 NIV

One of the most heartbreaking realities about turning sex into an idol is the damage it creates. In relationships that are supposed to be characterized by love, idolatry does nothing but ruin and corrupt. Norm Wakefield said it like this: "You cannot love someone you idolize."[11] That statement is so spot-on! Once idolatry infiltrates our hearts or perspectives, it robs us of the ability to love others. God has designed the husband's role to be governed by love above all things. "Husbands love your wives..." is how Paul instructed the Ephesian Christians (Ephesians 5:25–33). As husbands, *love* is supposed to be our number one priority as to how we go about fulfilling our roles in a God-honoring manner. Our love is to be patterned after the way Jesus loves the church and gives Himself for her. Serving, sacrificing, nurturing, cherishing...these are some of the attributes Paul uses in that passage to describe the way Jesus loves His bride. But mark my words, once an idol has been developed in our hearts, sacrificing for

---

[11] Norm Wakefield, *Equipped to Love.*

and serving others goes right out the window. Our idol now is the thing we cherish. Our idol is now the thing we sacrifice to. Our idol is the thing we serve and worship. And consequently, our wife gets demoted and becomes a tool to make sure our idol is served.

When men make an idol out of sex, we unknowingly turn it into wrecking ball. Sexual sin destroys. It corrupts. It ruins things. Those of us who have struggled with sexual idolatry know this very well. My own sexual idolatry robbed my marriage of intimacy for thirty years. Sex was a constant source of discord and animosity. We would "go through the motions" of sexual intercourse but all the while it was rotten at the core because I had turned sex into an idol. There were so many times in my marriage when Judi would say to me, "I wish God never invented sex!" She knew that sex had become a wedge between us that drove us apart. It created not only friction but also distance between us.

The marriage relationship is not the only thing that gets damaged by sexual idolatry. There are many things that are touched by the destructive element of idolatry that end up ruined to some degree or another. In this chapter I want to highlight some of the areas of our lives that get damaged when we have sexual idolatry in our hearts. Our ship has been attacked, so to speak. Like in the show *Star Trek*, imagine yourself to be Captain Kirk and I will be Scotty giving you the damage report to the Starship Enterprise. So here goes, in my best Scottish accent...

Damage Report Item 1: Self

One of the things we do not fully understand is that sex out of its appropriate boundaries causes ruin and problems. We either have been convinced or have convinced ourselves that if we pervert God's design for sex that not only will it give us pleasure but also in some way, a benefit. Like Eve was tricked by the serpent in Eden, we are deceived into thinking sex "God's way" keeps something back from us. We are missing out. If we do things God's way it will deprive us of something... I am not sure what, but something!

And so, we pursue sexual immorality, first in our hearts and then in some outward manifestation. We are thinking of our own benefit and pleasure but do not realize that we actually shoot *ourselves* in the foot when we turn sex into an idol. The first item on the damage report is ourselves! Notice how this verse to the church in Corinth says it:

> Flee from sexual immorality. All other sins a person commits are outside the body, but whoever sins sexually, sins against their own body. Do you not know that your bodies are temples of the Holy Spirit, who is in you, whom you have received from God? You are not your own; you were bought at a price. Therefore, honor God with your bodies. (1 Corinthians 6:18–20 NIV)

The command to flee sexual immorality is an interesting one, right? Flee usually communicates the need to get away from something because it is extremely dangerous. Like a venomous snake or a bomb about to go off. Similar to soldiers engaged in battle when the enemy is about to overtake them and kill them…the cry goes out, "*Retreat!*" and so the soldiers flee. Paul is saying that sexual immorality is extremely dangerous to us, personally. And because it is such a threat, we are told to run as fast as we can in the other direction. It will damage you!

The question is exactly how does it damage you? Primarily, sexual sin has specific implication to your walk with the Lord. Jesus has bought your body with the price of His own body and blood. He has put His Spirit in your body which now makes you a temple which His Spirit dwells in. Our bodies are to be used to honor and serve Him. Sexual sins are self-serving and self-honoring. Because sexual sin causes us to do the exact opposite (please ourselves) of what we have been saved for (please God), it is a sin against our very purpose. It is a self-serving act which leads us to become self-focused and self-serving. Sexual idolatry creates a perspective best described as "sensual," meaning we live to please our senses. It is obvious how this severely damages our relationship with Jesus. In order to follow Him, we must be able to deny ourselves and take up our cross. If we have made an idol out of sex, we end up elevating the self instead of denying it.

We have entered a phase in our culture where there are all kinds of "new" disorders being discovered. Things that were never previously recognized as diseases or disorders keep popping up left and right. One of the more recent disorders which had gained prominence in our sexually obsessed culture is the diagnosis of being a sex addict. Like drunkards or drug abusers, people have become addicted to pornography, masturbation, and all things sexual. They cannot stop thinking about it or stop using pornography or stop masturbating. This is an ironic development because the sexual disorder which followed next in sequence is erectile dysfunction. The sex addict cannot get enough...the ED sufferer can't get it up enough.

Sexual addiction is a real scientific reality for people who have allowed sex to become idolized in their hearts. Pornography, masturbation, and intercourse all produce hormonal release in our bodies which impact the brain in similar fashion to drugs. The hormones oxytocin and vasopressin impact your brain more powerfully than morphine. This produces a real, physical "high" that produces real, physical pleasure. Even the simplest among us can do the math in this situation. Sexual activity makes me feel really, really good, so I'm going to do it again and again and again. The consequence of this activity (whether pornography, masturbation, or sex itself) has become not only a habit based on repeated activity, but also a habit based on a biological experience. Just like drugs, our bodies can become dependent on those hormones. In this case, the impact is said to be even greater because these experiences biologically impact your brain so that it rewires itself a little bit each time it occurs. In our minds a specific, neurological link to the memory of what caused our wonderful experience is created...a neurological pairing or bonding takes place—a biological sense of becoming "one" with the experience.

The misfortune here is that this neurological bonding was what God intended for sex in marriage. A husband and wife working together to create *for each other* as well as *in each other*, a bond in sexual fulfillment and intimacy which links them together. That gives us some deeper insight into the biblical phrase "the two shall become one." Admittedly, I am no biologist or scientist in any deep sense of the word and what I have just relayed to you is only because I read about it somewhere, but God is the Creator of all things. He has made us in every sense of the word—biologically, neurologically, chemically, physically, emotionally, and spiritually. We are wired the way we are because He did it that way…on purpose! He knew this stuff long before we discovered it and He wanted it to be like this. When we step outside of His appointed boundaries for sex, we end up damaging ourselves as a result.

Being addicted to something includes an aspect of losing control. Whatever we might be addicted to now begins to not only influence our thoughts and decisions but eventually begins to control them. For the Christian man, there is only supposed to be one thing that controls us: God. God's will as communicated to us through His Word and empowered in us by His Holy Spirit is supposed to be the dominating force in our lives. His is to be the ultimate influence over us and nothing else. Like Paul told the Church in Ephesus,

> Do not get drunk on wine, which leads to debauchery. Instead, be filled with the Spirit. (Ephesians 5:18 NIV)

This concept gives new meaning to being under the influence! The Holy Spirit is to be the influence which we are under the most… not something else that we are addicted to. Sexual idolatry can cause brain damage…literally! It can lead us into an addictive approach to sex where sex becomes the master and we become the slave.

Damage Report Item 2: Gender Relationships

Sexual sin does not only damage us and lead us into bondage. When we turn sex into an idol, we damage others and our relationships with them. Whether it is in fornication or adultery or if we bring that idol into our marriage, those relationships are negatively impacted by our sexual idolatry. This destructive element is seen not only in broken or damaged relationships but also in core issues like attitudes and perspectives. For instance, the way we as men can view or think of women in general. Sexual idolatry causes men to think of women not as people created in God's image but more as a means to an end. They are a tool useful in serving our idol. Women are now more of an object than they are a person.

Our society is currently on the heels of the #MeToo movement, where consciousness about sexual harassment, exploitation, and rape have been brought to light and given prominence in the public eye. Specific perpetrators and situations have been called to account and highlighted on the news. The likes of Bill Cosby and Harvey Weinstein and many other famous men who have exploited women for years are being accused, charged, dragged before the courts, and thrown in prison in order to get justice for women who have been harmed by their actions. Corporations are enacting new stricter sexual harassment standards to help protect women from being treated poorly. The PC police are everywhere, examining each and every statement people make for any hint of misogyny. And whether your political leanings think things have gone too far or not far enough, the truth of the matter still remains: men with ungodly perspectives about sex have a tendency to view or treat women as sexual objects instead of people. Men's view of women can be directly and indirectly influenced by idolatrous sexual attitudes.

Do not get me wrong, I am not saying that women are not sexual beings. We all are, both men and women. Men and women are created with physical attributes and differences, and some of them are specifically sexual in nature. I am not saying that men should not find women attractive physically. That expectation would be unreasonable, especially in light of how God has wired us. I am not even saying that men should not use physical attraction as a reason to consider entering into a romantic relationship that may lead to them becoming married. What I am highlighting is how, when a man begins to idolize sex, they will develop a perspective about women that considers their worth based less on "who" they are and more on "what" they are. A perspective where worth and value isn't determined by what kind of person they are but rather if they physically or sexually measure up. Sexual idolatry causes us to lose connection with how true beauty is defined and displayed. We end up succumbing to a cultural standard of beauty rather than a biblical one. And we will lose the ability to relate to members of the opposite sex free from sexual thoughts and temptations.

This reality can occur even in our marriages. Husbands with sexual idols may even base their own wife's worth or value on standards in line with their idol. Physical beauty and sexual attractiveness may determine what he thinks about his wife. His value of her may decrease as she ages or puts on weight. His assessment of her value might depend on how she performs sexually. After a few children have left their marks on her, the idolatrous husband may wish he could trade her in for a younger model. As the years press on, he may begin to compare her with other women. Even physically attractive women will eventually lose in that contest. There is always a more attractive woman out there! Lord help us if we determine the value of our wife through eyes which view sex as an idol. That vision is severely tainted and will cause us to depreciate something that has exquisite value.

There is a good reason God commanded men not to covet other men's wives. Coveting will rob us of appreciation and thankfulness for what we have. The discontentment we will develop toward our wife will cause us to fail in our obedience to God to love our wives as Christ loves His church (Ephesians 5) and lead us to deal treacherously with the wife of our youth (Malachi 2:14). A sexual idol will damage even the basis for our "loving" relationship with our wife.

Damage Report Item 3: The Marriage Bed

One of the main areas a sexual idol will wreak havoc is in our bedrooms. My own idol robbed my wife and I of thirty years of sexual blessing. God intended sex to draw my wife and I into a oneness and intimacy which could not occur on account of how my heart idolized sex. Even though I would experience physical orgasm through our sexual activity, my heart was never satisfied. I brought unrealistic expectations to the bedroom which could never be fully satisfied. I "knew" how often sex should occur. I "knew" how my wife was supposed to engage sexually. I "knew" what sounds and looks and reactions my wife ought to respond to me with. I "knew" all these things ahead of time. And even though I could physically climax during our times of making love, emotionally I was left unsatisfied. My idolatrous concepts were insatiable. My frustrations could not be placated because I was convinced the only way to make me happy was if she lived up to the sexual imagery I desired. I was unaware that this expectation was and always will be an impossibility. And as a result, nearly every sexual encounter left me feeling as if something was missing instead of feeling amazed at what we had just shared!

Not only was it impossible for my wife to live up to my expectations; it was also not biblical. God had never intended sex to be what I had made it into. My sexual idol was not God honoring! As ironic as it sounds, I brought God into the mix regularly to defend my expectations. I knew God intended sex to be a regular blessing to my marriage. I wholeheartedly embraced the notion that God created sex for His people who were willing to enter faithfully into a lifelong covenant relationship with that one special woman for their entire lives. As a pastor, I had taught others that Christian husbands and wives were to be the people who experienced and enjoyed sex the most because that was what God intended from the get-go. Believe me, I knew all the verses to quote in order to support those ideas... I had those passages memorized and marked out in my Bible! Here are some of them:

> And they were both naked, the man and his wife, and were not ashamed. (Genesis 2:25 NKJV)

> Wives submit to your husbands as to the Lord...as the church submits to Christ, so also wives should submit to their husbands in everything. (Ephesians 5:22–24 NKJV)

> For this is the way the holy women of the past who put their hope in God used to adorn themselves. They submitted themselves to their own husbands, like Sarah, who obeyed Abraham and called him her lord. You are her daughters if you do what is right. (1 Peter 3:5–6 NIV)

> But a married woman is concerned about the affairs of this world—how she can please her husband. (1 Corinthians 7:34 NIV)

And this one was probably my favorite:

> Let the husband render to his wife the affection due her, and likewise also the wife to her husband. The wife does not have authority over her own body, but the husband does. And likewise, the husband does not have authority over his own body, but the wife does. Do not deprive one another except with consent. (1 Corinthians 7:3–5 NKJV)

These are just a few of the verses I used *against* my wife in response to whether she was sexually pleasing to me or not. Let me say now that I do not bring up these verses for you to develop an arsenal of biblical passages to use against your wife to get them to live up to your sexual expectations. I am bringing them up to confess that this is exactly what I did to my wife! Judi had to endure numerous "mini-sermons" from her loving husband about her failure to live up to my idolatrous standards. And if I did not actually pontificate on her deficiencies, she had heard enough of these lectures to know what my frustrated silence communicated. The message was clear: she was not good enough![12]

---

[12] I have counseled many men to do what I have tried to put into practice in my own life: read our own mail! Those verses about submission which were written

It is amazing how our sinful natures can take even what is holy and make it impure. The idol in my heart saw the Bible as a chisel to use against my wife to fashion her into what I wanted her to be sexually. And instead of washing her with the water of the Word, I repeatedly injured her with it.

I have spent some very tearful moments with my wife seeking her forgiveness for ruining so much of our marriage. As I said earlier, it was no less than thirty years of frustration, anger, arguing, cold shoulders, and disappointments which were caused by my idolatry. We missed out on thirty years of figuring out our sexual unique-ness in ways which could have drawn us closer and increased our love for each other. Thirty years of missing out on the learning and growing that working through the physical element of our marriage could have brought us. Think of all the communication and grace and learning from our mistakes that we lost out on. All the times we could have been talking it through—what pleased her, what pleased her more, what pleased her best! Learning and avoiding what did not please her at all. All the willingness to accommodate and sacrifice for each other, experiment and investigate, live and learn—together!

The fun of that journey was replaced with frustration and divi-sion. It makes me so sad to know that my sinful desires, which were built on the world's lies about sex, those sinful desires stole from us. They stole precious time which can never be recaptured. And even though we have now entered into a renewed love life, I have deep regrets for the ruin which sexual idolatry has brought to our marriage bed.

Unfortunately, ours is not the only marriage which has suffered on account of sexual idolatry. Many men bring this idol into their bedrooms. You may even be one of them. We might imagine that Christian marriages would be immune to this reality but that is just not so. Being a Christian does not make us immune to deception. As

---

for wives are their mail. Memorizing my wife's mail and lecturing her about her mail and beating her over the head with her mail has never helped my wife. If I want to help her become who God desires her to be, the best way I can help is by reading my own mail and putting God's instructions to me into practice in my own life.

a matter of fact, deception is one of the things Jesus warned His disciples against the most. Do not be deceived... You can be deceived! You can believe something that is not true. You can develop desires and thoughts that run contrary to God's Word and God's design. This is not a unique problem that I have developed in my own life. Paul spoke of this reality to the Corinthian church when he said,

> No temptation has overtaken you except what is common to mankind. (1 Corinthians 10:13 NIV)

I know that mine is not the only marriage which has had to deal with this issue. The idolization of sex has impacted many marriages. And it will continue to do so, as long as sex retains its position as an idol in our hearts.

As you were reading through the struggles which my wife and I have endured, it may have come to your mind that you are in the same boat I was. You can relate to the same frustrations I had. Perhaps your wife can relate as well! A vast amount of joy has been stolen from our marriage beds on account of sex being made into an idol. Men have pressured their wives to measure up sexually to expectations that they never can. Wives are living out their roles unaware that they are being held up to an impossible standard. "I don't measure up and I don't know why" is a thought many wives wrestle with. "Why can't I please my husband sexually?" they have asked themselves. Sexual idolatry creates a setting where they can never measure up or totally please their husbands.

And it can get even worse than that. Husbands with sex as an idol can treat their wife very poorly. Women have been coerced, manipulated, and even forced into performing in the bedroom beyond what their consciences would allow. They have been made to engage in certain sexual behaviors which turn their stomachs. Their husbands, who have been instructed to love them as Christ loves the church, have displayed that "love" in ways which are completely unloving, inconsiderate, and self-centered. Husbands regularly use the Word of God, playing the "I'm the head" card in order to manipulate their wives into submitting to and serving an idol. They unknowingly lead them into idolatry rather than "what is fitting in the Lord."

Keeping the marriage bed pure is God's idea. Keeping the devil and the world out of our bedroom is God's idea. Keeping sex "idol free" is God's idea. Part of the deception included with the lies we believe about sex is that God's ideas will not bring us true satisfaction or fulfillment. I believed that lie for a long time. I believed that what the world experiences in the sexual realm is better than what God could create in my own bedroom. Boy, was I wrong!

Damage Report Item 4: Testimony

Before I conclude this "damage report," I want to make sure we do not overlook one major area which has suffered great loss on account of this idol. There is collateral damage which has occurred that could be the most destructive aspect that sexual idolatry achieves. If we really think about it, this is probably the main objective Satan is out to accomplish as he schemes to pervert sex in our minds. That objective is to ruin our testimony and to make Jesus look bad.

As a man and wife interact with each other, as their relationship grows and develops, it takes on an aura which others around them can pick up on. Our marriages emit a spirit about them which others can sense and feel. The dynamic of our marriage paints a picture, so to speak. And the picture our marriages are supposed to create is an image which reflects the deep loving relationship Jesus has with His bride.

The Bible teaches us that from the beginning, God has intended our marriages to be a living representation to those around us of Christ and His bride, the church. Check out these verses:

> "For this reason, a man will leave his father and mother and be united to his wife, and the two will become one flesh." This is a profound mystery—but I am talking about Christ and the church. (Ephesians 5:31–32 NIV)

Back as far as the garden of Eden, God set up a system embedded in human relationships which would subliminally communicate a deep spiritual reality that points people in the direction of Jesus. In the garden is where God declared that a man would set aside the most important relationships in his life in order to establish a more important one. There in the garden is when God established that a husband and wife would become an inseparable entity...best of friends, closest companions, buddies for life. And there in the garden of Eden, in that inaugural statement about marriage, the sexual element of their relationship is highlighted with the declaration that sex would bring unity to those who enjoyed it. All of this was God's design and plan, and all of it was specifically designed. But why? Why did God do it that way? To help the world see Jesus better.

The institution of human marriage includes a profound mystery linking it to the spiritual reality of Jesus "marrying" the church. Everything about it was meant to communicate that reality clearly. When we mar any element of our own marriages, we scribble on the canvas where God wants us to paint a masterpiece. This includes our sexual life. The marriage bed is to be pure, free from sinful, worldly, or demonic influence. When we set up sex as an idol, it ruins the picture. The resulting frustration and division associated with that situation does not run parallel with the love Jesus has for His bride. His is a giving love. His is a love which overcomes what separates. His is a love which works with flaws and difficulties without allowing them to diminish His love for and acceptance of His bride. His love is characterized by patience. His is an enduring love which lasts into eternity. Husbands that idolize sex do not relate to their brides in a manner that reflects the love of Christ.

A great marriage speaks volumes. "*There's nothing better than a great marriage, and nothing worse than a bad one!*" I cannot remember who said those words, but they have always stuck with me. The marriage that experiences sex as the blessing God intended it to be preaches a great sermon! This kind of marriage emanates joy and peace and love and intimacy that others can sense. Sexual idolatry causes our marriage to preach a lame sermon. Our marriage can cause others to think poorly about Christ. And that is the worst damage of all.

Conclusion

I am sure once Captain Kirk received Scotty's "damage report," he would understand how dire the situation is. You cannot pilot a severely damaged ship for long before you have got to stop for repairs or end up broken down in some remote galaxy. I hope you see the severity of the situation so you can get to work on the repairs as well. There is never a hopeless case when God is in the mix. As always, our hope is built on Him, His will, and His ways. Our sexual idolatry may have resulted in some serious damage, but dealing with our sins is one of God's specialties! Get committed to thinking and acting according to God's ways and He can do some incredible repair work!

CHAPTER 5

COME TO LIGHT

You shall not make for yourself an image in the form of
anything in heaven above or on the earth beneath or in the
waters below. You shall not bow down to them or worship
them; for I, the LORD your God, am a jealous God.

—Exodus 20:4–5 NIV

God is a jealous God. There is no use debating the truth of that statement for He clearly says so in the Ten Commandments. It can be little disturbing to think about a negative emotion like jealousy being attributed to God, but He means what He says. He is jealous. And the interesting thing is He makes that statement in the direct context of commanding His people not to engage in idolatry. We typically understand jealousy to mean "wanting something someone else has," so what could God possibly be jealous of? Does He not already own everything? What does He want that someone else has? And what does this have to do with idolatry?

Let's answer the question in reverse. Let's not start with what does God want from us but rather what does He want to be for us. What does God desire to be for us? He wants to be our everything! He wants to be our Savior, our Leader, and our Provider. He wants us to find our strength and purpose and fulfillment in Him. He wants to bless our lives by directing our paths and guiding us into what is good and right. He wants to prevent our harm and protect our souls.

God desires us to find ourselves in Him. He wants to be so much to us. He wants to be our everything!

Think about idolatry in its most primitive sense. A jungle tribe has a statue in a shrine in their village. They serve it by saying their prayers to it. They present the statue with offerings of incense or food or some other things of value to them. There is worship and service given to that statue by everyone in the village. The question I want you to consider is why? Why do they offer sacrifices to that statue? What do they hope to gain from engaging in those behaviors? Ultimately, they want that statue to provide something for them! Maybe what they are looking for is a successful hunt or their crops to do well. Perhaps what they desire is to make it through the winter without someone in their family dying. Maybe someone in their family is sick and they are hoping the idol restores their health. There might be a man whose wife is having trouble getting pregnant. There are any number of desires these primitive tribesmen are looking for their idol to satisfy. They see worship of the idol as the means by which they will get the idol to give them what they want! If we dig deep enough, we will find that all idol worship is really, at its core, self-worship. What we want...what we desire is the driving force behind all idolatry. We want to please ourselves.

But remember, God desires to be the One in whom we find ourselves. He intends us to look to him for our fulfillment and purpose and joy and peace in life. He wants to be the One who provides us with all we need. He has set Himself up as the means through which our life comes to us, when it comes to us, how it comes to us, what is right, what is wrong, what is good and holy. We have been created by God to enter into that relationship with Him where He is everything to us. We have been created to worship and serve Him.

Christians throughout the centuries have developed statements of faith and catechisms in order to help us realize and understand what we believe, you know, what the Christian faith teaches us. And the catechism that addresses this particular point of discussion seeks to answer the question "What is the chief end of man?" The correct answer? "To glorify God and enjoy Him forever!" Kudos to you if you knew that one. Glorifying and enjoying God is at the heart of the purpose behind why God created us! We have been created to glorify Him and enjoy Him. How do we do that? The answer to that question can fill many chapters in many books (just ask John Piper!). But what I have been just describing may be a nice little summary of that answer. When Jesus is our everything, we will glorify Him and enjoy Him always.

So what is the problem? Why do we need the commandment to not engage in idolatry? I think one of the issues has to do with a sentence I included a little bit ago. "He has set Himself up as the means through which our life comes to us, when it comes to us, how it comes to us, what is right, what is wrong, what is good and holy." God is the One who determines the way things ought to go in our lives…when, where, how, etc…. But we want certain things and we want them when we want them. We want to determine how we get them, when we get them, and through whom they come. We want a say in the process and the timing. We have desires that we are afraid God will not fulfill. Or maybe we think He will not fulfill them *when* we want them fulfilled. That is when we begin to think about something or someone else being the source of those things God should be the source of. An idol is something that takes God's place in our lives. It is something we look to other than Him to give us what He alone should provide.

The reality of the situation is that anything can be an idol. A thing, a person, a situation or circumstance…an idol can be anything. People make money into an idol. Success and recognition can become idols. Well-behaved children or a family that has it all together can become idols (this is a big one in the homeschool community). You name it, our sinful hearts can give a "created thing" the place in our hearts that God alone is supposed to have. Young ladies might begin to think they cannot be fulfilled without getting married. Young wives can think she has no purpose unless she has a baby. We like to attach purpose and significance and meaning and fulfillment to things other than God and then convince ourselves we cannot have purpose and significance and meaning and fulfillment unless we have those things. All the while we forget that our purpose is found in God. Our significance and meaning come from our relationship with Him. He alone can fulfill and satisfy us because that is the way we have been created: to find our satisfaction in Him. And whether we chase our idols and never acquire them or get what we are after only to find it did not fulfill us the way we thought it would, an idol will always disappoint.

An idol in the heart of man steals away the affection and devotion we owe only to our Creator, Savior, and Lord. "Stuff of earth competes for the allegiance I owe only to the Giver of all good things."[13] We owe God our allegiance. We owe Him our hearts. We owe Him our devotion, our service, our worship...our everything! Every breath we breathe is a gift from God in heaven. Every good we experience comes to us through the channels of His amazing grace. We deserve nothing good from God, and yet He showers us with good regularly. He is to be thanked and praised and worshipped for being such a good God. When we give our affections to an idol, it makes God jealous. We have given our desires to something else He created instead of the Creator who made us.

When we have made anything in our lives into an idol, it makes God jealous!

Testimony Time

My idolatry stole from my devotion to the Lord. I was unaware of how much I had allowed the Creator's throne in my heart to be usurped by a created thing. I have repeatedly committed myself to serve God in every area of my life and I believe I meant it. I knew, and still know, that being a husband is one of the many opportunities I have be presented with for honoring and worshipping the Lord. I knew that loving my wife like Christ loved the church is worship. Every aspect of my role as a husband (making love included) presents me with another way I can honor God. It gives me another reason I can thank Him.

But instead of making me thankful for sex in my marriage, my idolatry made me upset. I wondered why God was not blessing me in

---

[13] "If I Stand," from the album *Songs* by Rich Mullins.

the sexual aspect of our marriage. I wondered why He would give me a wife who hated sex. I pleaded with Him to fix her. Because I had devoted my life to serve Him in any way, I could not understand why He would not change her heart about this. I ignored the promptings of His Spirit that maybe it was my heart that needed to change. Every inner struggle and frustration I experienced was an indicator that something was wrong with my own heart, but I would not consider that possibility. I reasoned that God should change her and everything would be fine. But because He did not, my frustration began to get directed at Him. The whole situation kind of reminds me of what it says in James 4:3:

> When you ask, you do not receive, because
> you ask with wrong motive, that you may spend
> what you get on your pleasures.

It was as if God was saying to me, "You have decided to serve this idol, but I certainly won't!" Like the old Keith Green song, "You pray to prosper and succeed, but your flesh is something I just can't feed."[14] I had the gall to ask God to serve my idol and He would not comply. The nerve!

My idolatry also stole from my devotion to my wife. It redirected my mind and affections in a way that resulted in me focusing on sex more than what honored God and blessed my wife. It gave sex the power to pick away at my ability to show love to my wife. How she "performed" in bed now had the power to change the enjoyment of the moment into something to be critiqued and judged. Like a judge in an Olympic event holding up scorecards after every sexual encounter we had, this idol would evaluate our love life, comparing it to the promises it had convinced me sex should include. Not only that... Those low scores on the judges' cards would create a resentment that seeped into other areas of our relationship. I would withdraw from her and become distant. I would help her less around

---

[14] "To Obey is Better than Sacrifice," from the album *No Compromise* by Keith Green.

the house. I would be less compassionate toward her difficulties and struggles. When she wanted to have conversations, I would not be very attentive. Little things about her that normally were no big deal would now irritate me. I would let more responsibilities attached to our home or our children rest on her shoulders. These are just a few of the ways my idol robbed my wife of the love I was instructed to show her. This list does not even include our frequent quarrels that would regularly surface when I got offended sexually. Those arguments often ended with her in tears, feeling like a failure and me feeling justified, hoping that this time it would change her!

Through the years I became convinced that the reason we did not enjoy sex the way God intended for us was because of her. Judi was the problem, plain and simple. She rejected me too often. She did not like sex. She was physically distant. She lacked passion. She was damaged goods. I blamed her. Sometimes I would couch my thoughts in veiled accusations. Sometimes I would blame her openly. Which approach I used was based on the level of my frustration. I could not be convinced that I was the source of the problem; it had to be her! And as long as it was her, I could avoid dealing with the issue that lay at the heart of the problem: me!

Thankfully God decided enough was enough. The Bible says, "Be sure that your sin will find you out," and my sin eventually found me out.

Like I said before, pornography was readily available to me as I was growing up. From my first experience at nine or ten with that magazine at my friend's house until I got saved when I was eighteen, pornography was a regular part of my life. When I reached puberty, my use of it had reached epic proportions. I was masturbating on a daily basis (sometimes more than once a day) and pornography was my regular companion for such activities. When I started sleeping with my girlfriend, that changed a little bit, but not as much as some might think. I used pornography regularly, even when I could have sex in real life. I guess you could say, old habits die hard and old friends are hard to say goodbye to.

When Jesus came into my life, He did some major house cleaning in every room and closet you can possibly imagine. As the Holy

Spirit led me through the New Testament, it was like God had written each and every letter for me. The Bible came alive as I read it and had the specific result of highlighting all the sins which I regularly committed. I had a great deal of trash I needed to throw out, including my sexual immorality. For me this meant I had to tell my girlfriend I would no longer sleep with her and I confessed my pornography use to mature Christians in my life. Pornography and fornication were cast aside, and I endeavored to keep myself pure sexually.

Eventually my girlfriend became my wife and we started a family together. Pornography and masturbation were left behind as part of my "old man" behaviors and replaced with the "new man" activity of biblically sanctioned sex with the wife of my youth. Sex now was only with my wife, never with myself, and deliverance from fornication and pornography was a part of my testimony. Little did I know that though I thought I was free from pornography, I was not quite free from what it had done to me. It had left some pretty wicked seeds in my mind which had grown into a perspective about sex which was not godly. No doubt, there were always temptations to remember stuff I had seen or read, which I tried hard to not do. There were always temptations to start using pornography again, which my will power gave me enough strength to resist. There were movies and shows that I watched which required me to fast-forward certain scenes or shut the movie off altogether. The reality is that there is always the presence of temptation in the world we live in that make it hard for a man to remain sexually pure. However, I was pretty sure that I was doing a good job at it. And other than the sexual frustrations I experienced with my wife, I was pretty confident that sex was in its appropriate boundaries in my life.

My wife and I have nine children together, which obviously indicates that we have had sex once or twice. (For those of you who want to ask, yes, we have finally figured out what causes pregnancy!) When people ask about why we have so many children, I like to make the most of the opportunity. I usually say, "We don't have a television set, so nights get a little boring" or "We don't have heat in our house, so we have to do something to stay warm." Four or five of our children are born in July, so eventually Judi told me I had to sleep on the couch the whole month of October!

I say all of this to highlight that well-known dynamic that things can appear right from the outside looking in but still be desperately wrong underneath the surface. And I had some things wrong on the inside.

A couple of years ago after another night of being turned down sexually, I decided to give in to some temptations that had been mounting. Judi had dozed off early and I was left to myself and my computer. There was not much for good shows available to watch on our streaming service, so I decided to get on the internet to see what was available for my viewing pleasure. Like I said previously, when we fall, we do not fall far. I had been secretly feeding my sexual idolatry for many months prior to this moment. Little by little I had been choosing entertainment which included more inappropriate sexual content. I had eliminated the practice of skipping scenes I should not watch. I had developed a sense of being "alone" as my wife slept in the bed next to me (with my finger on the appropriate button just in case she stirred). Spiritually speaking, all the pieces were in place for me to fall. That night I decided to "check out" what was available online.

As many of you know, pornography is available online. I knew that. And not only did I find some; I drank it in. I clicked from one video to another for quite some time that night. The supply seemed endless, and the more I watched, the less I wanted to stop. I knew I was sinning, but what the heck... If God was not going to fix my wife, then what was I to do? I had to satisfy this longing that God was obviously not going to satisfy for me. I had an appetite that my wife was obviously never going to feed. I knew there were women out there who enjoyed sex the way they were supposed to, and I wanted to experience that even if it was only by watching, even if they were only acting.

I cannot tell you how long I was online that night, but I can tell you that the Holy Spirit would not let me get away with it. The conviction was strong, and I knew I had to come clean. The next day I confessed my failure to my wife. I suppose that I inwardly hoped that a quick apology from me and a "This is probably my fault. I forgive you." from her would be all that was necessary to cover the incident.

Thankfully, my wife was too upset for that; otherwise I might still have this idol in my heart. She could not even discuss the situation with me for quite some time because she was so upset. I promised to do all the necessary things to make it right, I would get the right apps for my devices, I would confess it to others, I would get an accountability partner, I would even step down from ministry if necessary. I wanted to convince her that I was sincere in my repentance. I suppose I wanted to convince myself that I was sincere too. I knew what repentance was supposed to look like so I could go through the motions well enough. I am not so sure I was as sincere at that point as I thought.

I am so glad that one of the things which was included in my repentance was to get counseling. My wife and I do biblical counseling as a part of our ministry to others and we could both see that this was a situation where I needed to speak with someone about what was going on.[15] It was not long after my counselor had me pouring through the Scriptures and studying what God has to say about sex that God opened my eyes to see that my heart had made sex into an idol. I repented again to Him and I repented again to my wife. This time, it was the real thing! I sobbed and sobbed over what I had done—what I had done to my relationship with God, what I had done to my relationship with her. I cried about how for thirty years I had ruined our love with my perverted view of sex. I begged her forgiveness for blaming her for our problems when all along they were my fault. I tried my best to express the regret I felt inside for ruining the first thirty years of our love life on account of the idol in my heart. I knew I could not change the past or remove the pain I had caused and that the only way we could move past it was if she would forgive me. I pleaded with her that she would forgive me so things could be the way God wanted them to be between us. And praise God, she did forgive me! And she still does!

Her forgiveness to me in that moment is one of my greatest joys in life. I was desperate for her to release me from the pain and misery

---

[15] Our training is from ACBC (formerly NANC) biblical counseling which focuses on the Scriptures as the sole basis for counseling as opposed to secular or integrative counseling.

I had caused our marriage. I knew I did not deserve it, but I knew it was the only hope our relationship had. I am so thankful that God put that grace in her heart after all I had put her through. After all the years of grief my idol had caused us, she could still forgive me! She saw the sincerity of my heart, broken before her with a willingness to turn from the sin that was polluting our marriage bed. She was willing to let go of what was in the past and move forward with me into what God could do in our marriage now that this idol was gone. What an incredible blessing forgiveness is! And what an incredible door of blessing her forgiveness opened in our marriage so we could walk into new depths of love and intimacy. God's plans are always best, and her forgiving me was a part of that plan!

Since God revealed this idol in my heart, and He has graciously assisted me in demolishing it, our marriage has grown incredibly! Judi and I love each other more deeply, are more patient and gracious toward each other, and enjoy sex more and more every time. Another "blessing" of my situation is that it has become the foundation for this book as well as my ministry to other men who struggle with the same issues I have. It is my prayer that God will make beauty from the ashes of my struggles and failures and maybe will prevent the long years of heartache which Judi and I have experienced from being what other marriages would face.

Discovering Your Own Idols

As I look back on my situation, I can recognize many different realities that, if I had known about, maybe would have helped me recognize my idolatry sooner. Though I was blinded to my idolatry, there were plenty of things present in my life that indicated that idol was there. I know I have the propensity to ignore these telltale signs and perhaps the knowledge of them would have done me no good, but I can hope that me pointing them out will help someone else. In Hosea 4:6 God says, "My people are destroyed from lack of knowledge." Perhaps the knowledge about these "idol indicators" will help prevent some destruction in your own marriage! These "idol indicator lights" are useful in identifying anything we may have turned into an idol, not only sex, and so they could be helpful for the discovery of any idol we may have. I will apply them to the topic at hand, but you can feel free to look for further applications other than just identifying sexual idols. I briefly mentioned some of these indicators in chapter 1, but I would like to flesh them out a bit more here.

Indicator Light 1

The first indicator light may be found in answering the question "Where do you run?" What I mean by that is, when you are facing times of stress or feeling the need to retreat, where do you go? What do you turn to when you are looking for a place to hide? If life is beating you up or got you down, what will solve your problems? For me, when I had a hard day or when I wanted to unwind, sex was the thing I desired most to bring that relief. My wife would regularly say to me, "Sex fixes everything for you, doesn't it?"

And I would reply, half joking, "Yes, it does!" Of course, that was not true. Sex does not fix everything.

I'm not kidding. It really doesn't!

It took God revealing my idol to me to convince me of that truth. Sex did not fix anything! The problems I had before sex were still there afterward. The things causing the stress in my life were ready to hit me again the next chance they got. The bills still were not paid, and the vehicles still needed repairs, but hey! At least for a little while I could forget about them.

I know there is not a whole lot wrong with a little bit of distraction from life's difficulties every now and then, but remember what idolatry is? An idol can be something, someone, or some situation other than God which we turn to in order to get what God wants to supply us. Does God want to be who we run to in our time of need? Yes! He wants to be our Shelter from the storm, our Strong Tower to which we flee when we feel threatened or overwhelmed. He declares that He will bring us peace and calm our spirits when they are anxious. Jesus says to the weary and heavy-laden, "Come unto me!" He invites us to cast all our cares on Him. Why? Because He cares for us!

He really does care for us and He wants to be the One we dump on, the One we vent to, the One we run to in our times of need.

I know just because we use things as distractions from life does not automatically indicate we have made that thing into an idol, but it could. If we find ourselves regularly turning to that thing to ease our pains, sufferings, anxieties, or fears, we might have set that thing up as an idol in our hearts. Some people do that with drugs, alcohol, or cigarettes. Some people do it with food, shopping, or entertainment. As I look back on my life, I can see that I did this with sex.

Indicator Light 2

That leads me to another indicator light for idolatry: pride. The fact that I could make love to my wife even though life was rough was a pride issue in and of itself. I imagined other men would find it difficult to make love to their wives if their minds were preoccupied with their difficulties. Judi used to say I would want it even if I was dying in the hospital. That made me proud! Though I might have felt that I did not necessarily have the stamina to be great at sex, I was sure I could have sex often. If we made love more than once in a day, or if I could convince Judi to go again for a third time, I felt proud that I could rise to the challenge. But my pride was based on an idolatrous notion that increased frequency was an aspect of what "good" sex was supposed to include. Pornography had taught me that good sex included thinking about it all the time and doing it as often as possible. And my pride aligned with what my idol taught me.

The presence of pride in our lives should always be a warning sign. Very rarely is pride appropriate. Allow pride to send you into your thoughts to see what its source is, and when you find that source, root it out the second you find it! It could indicate the presence of an idol!

Indicator Light 3

Preoccupation is another indicator. When an idol sets up house in our hearts, it draws attention to itself, expecting you to give it a lot of time and consideration. Because an idol can only get set up in our hearts with our permission, we willingly give it the attention we think it deserves. Our thoughts and affections are given to whatever our idol is. If we examine what we regularly give our attention to, we might discover how much of an influence our idol has in our lives. It slowly seeps its way into other areas of who we are. It looks for ways it can get incorporated into other aspects of our lives. In other words, one of the indicating factors that reveal that something has become an idol is that we give our attention to it outside of its appropriate boundaries.

Men who have turned sex into an idol might make sexual jokes or innuendos in regular conversation. We may pervert innocent words others say and turn them into sexual things in our minds, sometimes even speaking those thoughts aloud. We might discuss sexual things with people we should not. Men with this idol can begin to turn just about anything sexual. This goes beyond the dynamic of a teenage boy trying to contend with his hormones flaring up. This is an ungodly preoccupation with sex, expressing the reality that it has crossed its God-ordained borders.

Indicator Light 4

Finally, I want to give you one of the best litmus tests I have found which will help indicate an idol has taken up residence in your heart. This is indicator light 4. First let me start by saying, just because we have a desire in our life, it does not necessarily mean we have made that thing into an idol. Desires in and of themselves are not wrong or sinful. Desires can become idols if we want what we want too much or in a way which does not honor God. But how can we tell if our desires have crossed that line? What can help any of us know if a desire has turned into an idol?

Here are two questions to assist in determining if we have made our desires into idols:

1. Am I willing to sin to get it?
2. Do I sin if I do not get it?

I cannot remember who came up with this litmus test because I sure would like to give them credit for it. I am fairly certain I heard it in one of our counseling training sessions, but I am not totally sure. Regardless of that, the test is very useful in weeding out idols. Am I willing to sin to get what I want? Do I sin as a result of not getting it? In other words, does not having my desire met lead me to dishonor or disobey God?

In regards to sex becoming an idol, it's not too difficult to see how this works itself out. Fornication is an obvious example. We want sex and we are willing to sin to get it. We engage in sexual behavior outside of God's appointed boundaries for it. We are either unwilling to make the commitment to the lifelong covenant of marriage, or we are unwilling to wait until we are married to have sex. Because we idolize sex, we sin against God and transgress His command to experience sex the way He ordained.

But what about after we are married? How does this dynamic play out in that setting? Let me highlight the answer to the first question (Am I willing to sin to get it?) from personal examples. In order to get sex, I had turned many of the ways I could display love to my wife into "bargaining chips" in order to coerce or manipulate a future willingness on her part. I would do nice things during the day in order to secure her favor in the bedroom later on. Instead of pitching in with household chores because it was the right thing to do, much of my "helping out" came with strings attached. Vacuuming the living room or doing the dishes were not acts of kindness; they were ways to make Judi indebted to me. Sometimes she might ask me for a favor, and I would say something like, "I'll make you a deal…" And usually that deal meant I would only be nice to her if she promised to make love to me later.

Can you see what I am trying to highlight? My idolatry contaminated our regular interactions. Things which could have been tangible expressions of my love for her were essentially selfishly motivated behaviors intended to control her. And even though that was not always the intention every time I did something nice, it made each act of kindness something to be suspicious of. Was I being nice or out to get something? Was I being loving, or did I just want her to do something for me? If Judi wanted to, she could legitimately ask the question, "Does what you have done show me that you love me, or that you love sex?" I am ashamed to admit that all too often the honest answer would have been that I loved sex.

And what about the second question? Did I sin if I did not get what I want? I am sure you already know the answer to that question! I have already discussed that reality, but I want to highlight it again here to show how this indicator light works.

I would react to Judi's rejection of me in sinful and very often childish ways.

There were certain times in our lives I would come to bed expecting to make love. For instance, there were many times I would feel justified to expect Judi to make love to me. If I had performed all the necessary acts of kindness and good deeds to make her indebted to me, if it had been "too long" since our last encounter, if she had just finished her period and we had to make up for lost time, if I had secured a "deal" based on an earlier agreement—lots of reasons were present in my mind that convinced me, I had it coming! And believe me, if she failed to keep up her end of the bargain, I would be upset. If she was not in the mood or too tired (why a mother of nine children would ever be too tired to make love to her husband, I have no idea!), I might not have been as understanding as I ought. There were certain times when I would expect sex simply because it was the right day of the year! Anniversaries, Valentine's Day, my birthday, date nights, any type of celebratory event, whatever sounded like it should include some level of romance or physical enjoyment might develop in me the expectation that she should not say no tonight. And if she disappointed me, well, I would be frustrated. It would upset me. Sometimes I would be angry. Sometimes I would be very angry!

If I was upset, I had a few "go-to" behaviors which would "communicate" my frustrations to her: short answers in conversations, leaving for work without kissing her goodbye, cold shoulder attitudes, leaving household responsibilities on her shoulders, going out of the way to avoid her. These were the "nicer" ways I handled my frustrations. The "meaner" things included arguments and fights or times when I did not guard my words from being insulting or demeaning. Remember what James said causes fights and quarrels? They come from us not getting what we wanted! That was true with lots of our fights about sex. I did not get what I wanted. Fighting was not the only way I expressed my desires going unmet; there would also be times that I blamed her for all the problems we had in the bedroom. In short, I would fail to love her the way Christ expected me to. And I would fail to resolve our conflicts in a way that pleased God. I handled the problem in a way that ultimately made the problem worse, proving the truth from Solomon's wisdom that our anger can make us do foolish things (Proverbs 14:17).

I realize that I am not the only man who sins when they are rejected sexually by their wives. Some of you are not as bad as I am, but some of you could be worse. Your anger might be displayed in verbal abuse or violence. Some of you might turn to pornography and masturbation. Others might go so far as to commit adultery. Though the degree to which we sin may be less or more sinful, the fact that we do sin is what I am trying to focus on. The specific sinful reaction is not necessarily the primary point, and I only bring them up to highlight the many possible ways the idols in our hearts reveal themselves. Do not miss the point by comparing your own sins to the sins of others or by justifying your sinful reactions. The reality of the situation is if we sin because of being disappointed sexually, it may reveal that we have turned sex into an idol.

Conclusion

Obviously, when sex becomes an idol, it does not paint a pretty picture. Idols can never bring a blessing to our marriages. They will only cause ruin and misery. Idolatry cannot bring us the peace and love and joy our marriages were intended to experience. The things of God's kingdom cannot come into our lives when we embrace what is forbidden. God is a jealous God, just as He says He is. He will not bless what He condemns. Notice what God says to Ezekiel:

This is what the Sovereign LORD says:
When any of the Israelites set up idols in their

hearts... I the LORD will answer them Myself in keeping with their great idolatry. (Ezekiel 14:4 NIV)

You can bet that God's "answer" in response to idolatry in the heart is not a pleasant one! If we do not recognize those things in our lives which we have turned into idols, and deal with them properly, we should only expect things to go poorly. As long as sex remains an idol in your heart, sex will only frustrate and anger you. It will rob your marriage of God's blessing. It will continue to make you fail to love your wife and treat her as Jesus commands you to.

God alone deserves to be enthroned on the altar of your hearts. Allow those indicator lights to shine a spotlight on the idolatry in your own heart, and when God's Spirit does reveal an idol, tear it down! Rip it to the ground and get it off the altar.

That is what we will talk about in the next chapter: tearing down the idol we have made of sex!

CHAPTER 6

DESTROYING SEXUAL IDOLS

And the Angel of the Lord appeared to him and said,
"The Lord is with you, you mighty man of valor!"
—Judges 6:12 NKJV

When it is revealed to us that we have an idol in our hearts, what are we to do? The story of Gideon presents us with some dramatic descriptions concerning what God instructed him to do about idol worship present among God's people. This specific incident concerning idol worship was present in his own backyard! In this one event, there are strong parallels to our discussion about sex being made into an idol. Gideon's story is one which I would like to use as a springboard to help us answer how we are to deal with the idol of sex which we have set up in our hearts.

Gideon lived in Israel at a time in their history when their country was under attack. Their nation was experiencing regular raids by enemies which would destroy or plunder their crops and livelihood. As a nation, the people cried out to God to deliver them from their enemies and God responded. God asked Gideon to do the job of deliverance and eventually used him to lead the people to victory over the Midianite marauders. However, *the real issue* was the situation which originally caused God to allow the Midianites to harass Israel to begin with. They had an idolatry problem which God wanted to deal with! In the story of Gideon there are certain elements which run parallel with the problem of sexual idolatry.

The first strong parallel I see in the Gideon account is that the idol he is being called to contend with was his father's idol. I do not think this is a coincidence. The reason I see this as a strong parallel to our discussion is because very frequently, men who deal with an inappropriate view of sex have inherited it, a family heirloom, so to speak. Many men from my generation who came across pornography at an early age did so because it was in their home. Books, magazines, and videos used to be the main medium for pornography. A lot has changed since I was a boy, but it used to be that in order to use pornography, you had to purchase it. Pornography was physically present in many of our homes because it had to be bought. That might not be the case anymore, but it was for me and for many of you. The primary reason I could use pornography as a child was because my dad had it. And because it was something he had to purchase, he kept it. I could sneak into his closet or dresser and find it hidden there. Because he had an issue with pornography, I had access to it. And as a result of my poking around and getting into his things, his problem became my problem.

That situation is not unique to me, either in a literal sense or in a spiritual one. In the direct context of the prohibition against idolatry, we are told that God will visit the iniquities of the fathers on to their children, even down to the third and fourth generation (Exodus 20:5). I admit that there is much debate about exactly what that means, but there is *at least* a reference to children being visited by their father's iniquities. In my somewhat simple mind, I think that means that the sins which our dads struggled with could become the sins we struggle with. Their iniquities visiting their sons. A lot of those iniquities do not only come for a visit but move in and stay our entire lives and often get passed down to our own sons!

Gideon was in that situation, right? God commanded Gideon to tear down the altar to Baal and the Asherah that was with it. And where was this altar to Baal and Asherah? In his father's yard. The idol in question was on their property. Apparently, their home had become a community place of worship where the town would come to offer their sacrifices to Baal and Asherah. And when Gideon tore down his idols, boy were the townsfolk hot! They were ready to kill whoever had desecrated what they worshipped. Thankfully, Gideon's father, Joash, came to his rescue by advocating that the people of the town let Baal get his own revenge against Gideon!

The next parallel in Gideon's story revolves around what type of idols Gideon was commanded to tear down. Those idols were images of the gods, Baal and Asherah. Who were these gods and what was involved in worshipping them? Most historians tell us that these religions believed that Asherah was the wife of the Canaanite god named El. El and Asherah were thought to be very passionately consumed with each other and gave birth to lots and lots of baby gods. Baal was one of their many sons. As time went by, Baal got a little too big for his britches and started overthrowing all the other gods. Eventually, Asherah abandoned her husband, El, and hooked up with her son Baal and they became the top dogs of the religions in that area. This puts them in some suspicious light as it pertains to their incestuous sexual relationship with each other, but what can you say? The gods do what they want, no?

Both Baal and Asherah were associated with fertility, and not only because of their sexual relationship. Baal was the storm god, associated with thunder and the rain, and Asherah was represented by a tree or a pole carved to look like a tree. Their association with fertility became the prominent aspects of why and how they were worshipped: Baal worshippers' mind-set was that the worship of Baal contributed to fertile soil fed by abundant rains which would mean good harvests. The worship of Asherah would lead to lots of fertility in the human reproductive sense of the word. Lots of crops and lots of kids meant prosperity to an agricultural society.

Not only that, but what Baal and Asherah represented as gods influenced *the way* people worshipped them. Along with the normal practice of animal sacrifice and divination, all kinds of sexual perversion, public sexual acts, and religious prostitution were regular aspects of Baal and Asherah worship. Because they were gods of fertility, sexual immorality was central in this type of idolatry. I am confident that you can see the association of these specific idols with our discussion concerning sexual idolatry!

The worship of Baal and Asherah was forbidden by God, both in the general sense of violating the first and second commandments, as well as in the definitive sense, when God repeatedly and specifically named them as gods of the land which Israel was not permitted to worship. And even though they were repeatedly and specifically warned against it, this type of idolatry plagued God's people throughout the entire Old Testament. As Matthew Henry put it (I'm paraphrasing a little bit), "A child once burned learns to fear the fire, but this perverse and unthinking people that had so often been punished for idolatry returned to it again and again."[16]

That leads me to my third parallel with this situation: sexual idolatry is to be constantly guarded against! For us men, we must regularly be on guard against the devil's attempts to mess us up in our view and approach to our sexuality. Israel's continual struggle with sex as an idol is a good reminder of how powerfully and relentlessly sexual immorality pulls at men's hearts. It also serves as a good warning concerning what lengths we must go to rid ourselves of it. We must constantly strive to keep our hearts sexually pure. Keeping our hearts pure of sexual idolatry will keep the marriage bed pure and lead to God's blessing upon it!

Tearing Down Sexual Idols

So what are you to do if an idol has found its way into your heart? What if the previous chapters describe you or your situation? Perhaps you grew up in a home where you had access to pornography. Maybe your sexual idolatry did not come from your dad, but you have that problem anyway. Make no mistake about it. Each of us has the capability to develop our own sexual idolatry without the help of our fathers! There is a strong chance that if you're reading this book, you have a struggle with sexual sin in your life that is a manifestation of the way you have turned sex into an idol in your heart.

---

[16] *Matthew Henry's Commentary on the Whole Bible* (Judges 6).

What should you do about it? How does God want you to handle the situation?

Let's start by looking at what God told Gideon to do with the altar to Baal and Asherah.

> That same night the LORD said to him (Gideon), "Take the second bull from your father's herd, the one seven years old. Tear down your father's altar to Baal and cut down the Asherah pole beside it. Then build a proper kind of altar to the LORD your God on the top of this height. Using the wood of the Asherah pole that you cut down, offer the second bull as a burnt offering." (Judges 6:25–26 NIV)

What do we do with the idol we have made out of sex? The short answer is: *Tear it down! Cut it to pieces! Throw it in the fire!* God's remedy for sexual idolatry is clear: destroy it completely.

This formula for Gideon's situation is helpful for us in dealing with our own. The situation is not perfectly identical but in principle it runs parallel. Allow me to elaborate. Gideon's situation had him dealing with a physical idol which was built on an altar that could be seen. And even though all idolatry is primarily a heart issue, his situation called for him to deal with an external reality: an actual altar, an actual idol, an actual shrine set up to worship a sexual idol. Gideon was instructed to destroy the *expression* of sexual idolatry. You and I need to confront the hidden enemy, an internal one. Our idol is invisible. It is unseen. It is hiding on the inside, deep in our hearts. However, very often in the Scriptures God speaks or acts in external expressions that speak to internal realities. In Gideon's instructions we have some external actions that point to inward realities. The way Gideon was commanded to deal with the external expression of sexual idolatry contains principles that point to inward steps we must take to rid ourselves of our own sexual idolatry.

If we have turned sex into an idol, we have sin in our hearts and lives, and when a Christian is faced with dealing with any sin in their lives, *the Bible only provides us with one approach in dealing with it: that we seek God's grace and forgiveness through repentance.* The tearing down of that idol is entirely wrapped up in that remedy. And if repentance is the only thing that tears down the idols in our hearts, then it is imperative that we understand what repentance is. We must not be fooled by counterfeit versions of repentance. If we are to receive grace and forgiveness and destroy this idol, we must repent—and repent fully!

So let's walk through the process of repentance to be sure we understand what it entails.

Biblical Repentance: Sorrow

Repentance begins with conviction of sin and the proper emotional response to it. In other words, we recognize that our sin is terribly wicked, and we feel terrible about it. Sorrow over sin is an ingredient in true repentance. There is a good example of that in the book of Acts,

> When the people heard this, they were cut to the heart and said to Peter and the other apostles, "Brothers, what shall we do?" (Acts 2:37 NKJV)

Those who heard Peter's message that day understood the depth of their need of God's forgiveness for their sins and were "cut to the heart." That indicates an inward emotional response to the recognition of their own sins.

The apostle Paul also recognized the importance of this emotional aspect of repentance. He had previously rebuked them for sinful behavior and noticed they responded with a godly sorrow that produced in them a true repentance (2 Corinthians 7:8–11). We will dig further into the details of what that godly sorrow looked like in a little while.

In the book of James, we also find instructions on what to do when we find a sinfulness in our hearts. Those instruction were as follows:

> Come near to God and He will come near to you. Wash your hands, you sinners, and purify your hearts, you double minded. Grieve, mourn and wail. Change your laughter to mourning and your joy to gloom. Humble yourselves before the Lord and He will lift you up. (James 4:8–10 NIV)

Grieve, mourn, and wail. Change your laughter to mourning and your joy to gloom. That sounds pretty descriptive concerning our emotional perspective about our sin.

The long and the short of it is this: when we are repentant, we feel genuine sadness about our sin. There is a sorrow that contributes to our repentance.

When I was confronted with my own sexual idolatry, I sincerely felt bad about it. As God revealed more and more of what my sinful heart had done with His good gift of sex, I felt more and more sorrow and brokenness over my wickedness. I was emotionally torn over viewing pornography. Not only that, but I was also broken because of what it had done to my relationship with God and my wife. I was sorry for the length of time this idol had been present in my life as well as the damage it had done through those years. This sorrow was an important element in leading me to repent of my immorality. As I said before, I sought forgiveness from God and my wife through many tears.

Having said that, repentance is much more than just feeling bad about our sin. As a matter of fact, we can feel bad about a great number of things and never truly repent of them. In the passage I referred to earlier in 2 Corinthians, Paul differentiates between a worldly sorrow and true godly sorrow. I want to dig into what he says there for a moment to highlight the differences between the two so we can be on guard against worldly in our own repentance. Look at how Paul addresses the Corinthians in these verses:

> I am not sorry that I sent that severe letter to you, though I was sorry at first, for I know it was painful to you for a little while. Now I am glad I sent it, not because it hurt you, but because the pain caused you to repent and change your ways. It was the kind of sorrow God wants His people to have, so you were not harmed by us in any way. For the kind of sorrow God wants us to experience leads us away from sin and results in salvation. There's no regret for that kind of sorrow. But worldly sorrow, which lacks repentance, results in spiritual death. Just see what this godly sorrow produced in you! Such earnestness, such concern to clear yourselves, such indignation, such alarm, such longing to see me, such zeal and such a readiness to punish wrong. You showed that you have done everything necessary to make things right. (2 Corinthians 7:8–11 NLT)

Paul wrestled with the dynamic of how blunt he had been in addressing the sin present in the Corinthian church in the letter he had previously sent them. That letter may have seemed harsh or hurtful in the way he confronted them about their sins, but ultimately it proved to be right and good for them. The proof was their response to Paul's rebuke—their godly sorrow which led them to repent of their sin. In his discussion about this sorrow, Paul shows that he was not exactly a naive Pollyanna who believed the best about every situation. He knew that their initial response could have been what he termed a "worldly sorrow" which would have had a bad result. He expressed that there was a marked difference between worldly sorrow and godly sorrow in response to sin. Let's see if we can highlight some of those differences.

Worldly Sorrow

First thing I want to say about worldly sorrow is that there is some actual sorrow. By that I mean to say people with worldly sorrow do *feel sorry!* But what are they sorry about? And what is the focus of their sorrow? Maybe they are sorry they got caught. Perhaps they are sorry that their sin has made things difficult for them. They might be sorry they cannot enjoy things like they did before they got caught. They are sorry they are in the doghouse because of what they did. They might even be sorry they have to deal with things because it would be easier for them if they did not have to.

If that is the type of grief you are experiencing, then you are in trouble! These "sorrows" are worldly because they are mostly focused on you! Worldly sorrow is self-focused and self-deceiving. We definitely "feel" bad, not about our sin but more about the way the consequences of our sin have negatively affect our lives. Because we "feel" some pain, we might be deceived into thinking we have some level of genuine repentance taking place. We might say the right things to make it sound like we mean to repent, but mostly we do it because it will make others think we are genuine. That way they will forgive us without us having to do the real work of repentance.

When I first was confronted with my own sexual idolatry, this was my inner hope. I hoped that if I said and did the right things that made it sound like I was truly repentant, my wife would respond with forgiveness and we could put it all behind us and I could keep pretending like nothing was wrong. That worldly approach would not truly address the sin in my heart. It would be like Gideon just building a wall in front of the altar to Baal and Asherah so people could not see that it was still there. That worldly approach would only hide the reality that the idol was in fact still in place and therefore it would never be truly torn down. God wants our idols torn down, and worldly sorrow does not do that. Worldly sorrow produces only a "false" repentance. There is nothing genuine in it which results in salvation and deliverance from the sin we are supposed to be repenting of. But godly sorrow leads to the demolition of idols God is looking to accomplish! It truly tears down idols in our hearts.

Let's see why as we examine what true sorrow that pleases God looks like.

Godly Sorrow

In his description of godly sorrow, Paul lists eight characteristics that mark what godly sorrow and true repentance involves. A quick examination of each of those characteristics might help us to see if they are present in us as we deal with our sexual idols.

- The first on the list is *earnestness.* This word has two main elements involved in its definition. The first is haste. Earnest means there is no procrastination involved in dealing with the sin God has convicted you of. The earnest penitent feels the need to deal with their sin sooner, not later. He does not put it off. The second idea is diligence, meaning we are seriously committed to do everything necessary to uproot our sinful idols, from start to finish. We are serious about dealing with our sin, and the sooner we get started, the sooner we are done.
- The next characteristic is the concern to *clear yourself.* This does not mean we are looking for an opportunity to explain or excuse our behavior but rather the willingness to be completely honest. We are willing to tell all if necessary. We can and will confess the specifics of our sin, even to the point of motives and intention. We can "explain" everything that is going on in our hearts and in our actions. If we need to go into details we will, just so it is all on the table and out in the open. It is like we have the attitude that says, "Let's deal with all of it so we don't have to revisit this moment again." This is what is really meant when people with godly sorrow say, "I just want to come clean." They want to confess it completely, not just parts. Vague confessions do not lead to freedom. "People do not change in fuzzy-land!"[17] The

---

[17] Brad Bigney.

person experiencing godly sorrow knows they need to be completely honest or else some root of that sin will remain hidden and start to resurface in their lives.

- The next thing is this feeling of *indignation*. The general definition of the word indignation means to experience anger because of injustice or wickedness. It is the feeling that we get when we hear about gruesome child abuse or some other type of abominable criminal activity. The feeling we experience in those instances that such a person deserves to be severely punished for their loathsome behavior is indignation. In our situation, indignation means we feel that way about our own behavior! We cannot believe we have stooped to such lows or sinned in such ways. We are indignant at ourselves for allowing an idol to be fashioned in our hearts. We realize there is no excuse for our sin and agree with God about how heinous our sin really is. Our indignation communicates that we know our behavior is worthy of justice and punishment. And though we desire and seek forgiveness and mercy, we can honestly express that we do not deserve it.

- In this version of the Bible (New Living Translation), they have chosen to use the word *alarm*. It comes from the Greek word *Phobos* which means "fear or terror." The English equivalent is the word phobia. Godly sorrow for our sin sees the harm which our sin can ravage on our souls. We can see and feel the negative impact our sin has on our relationship with God. It recognizes that our sin could have damaged our relationship with others beyond the point of repair. We are afraid that we did not deal with our sin soon enough and that we may reap the destruction which our sin brings with it. This "alarm" is one of the motivating factors behind us being quick to deal with it. We do not let it linger and allow it to wreak more havoc than it already has.

- The next characteristic is *longing*. This means godly sorrow develops a desire in our hearts that things will not stay the way they are for long. We really want things to be different, to be right. We want to move on in our lives into the place where God has always desired us to be. We truly wish for the damage our sin has done to be repaired so we can live our lives the way God intended.

- *Zeal* is next on Paul's list. Paul saw something in the Corinthian response to his rebuke that meant they had an inner enthusiasm about the sins he had confronted them about. Not that they were excited that they sinned, but that their godly sorrow gave them a drive inside to get to work on things. They were willing to do whatever is necessary to overcome their sin issues. They were "into it" as it pertained to the work of repentance. They were not just going through the motions of repenting, but their hearts were in it too.

- Near the bottom of the list we come across the phrase *"readiness to punish wrong."* In these words, Paul means to communicate that if we have true, godly sorrow, we understand there may be consequences for our actions. Our sin deserves to be punished, and if punishment is what comes for it, we can accept it. If we have hurt someone else in our sin, we understand if they do not want to forgive us. We realize that unless they choose for things to be reconciled between us, we cannot force that to happen or hold it against them. If there are other consequences which come our way, we receive them, knowing we truly deserve them. Our godly sorrow accepts the fact that *sin deserves judgment.* We can receive forgiveness but know that we do not deserve it. That perspective makes forgiveness so much more valuable to us when it finally comes!

- Finally, Paul says their godly sorrow created in them a *willingness to make everything right.* The word Paul used is often associated with purity or cleansing. It can mean "sacred," which indicates that godly sorrow looks to do whatever contributes to things being the way God wants. We want everything in the way we handle our sin to be pleasing to God. We desire to honor God in the fact that we are truly repentant for our sin and are that we are willing to do all we have to do to get and stay clean; we want to be right with Him and others whom our sin has harmed. Those relationships are sacred to us, and we want them to remain that way from now on.

What an incredible list! Digging into these descriptions paints a clear and obvious picture that repentance is much more than just feeling bad. As someone has said before, "Repentance isn't just when you cry, it's when you change!" These characteristics present in godly sorrow are the necessary ingredients which fuel the changes that must take place in our lives for our repentance to be considered genuine. Let's move on to discuss the primary offense present in all sin.

Biblical Repentance: Dealing with the Primary Problem of Sin

Sorrow is a necessary part of repentance, but it is not the whole. Repentance includes many other things. Before I move on to discuss those things, allow me to preempt that discussion by looking at Psalm 51:4:

> Against You only have I sinned and done
> what is evil in Your sight. (Psalm 51:4 NIV)

This Psalm is a record of King David's response when he was confronted about sins he had committed. He had gotten lazy, engaged in adultery, impregnated another man's wife, conspired to cover his sin by getting this man drunk so he would sleep with his wife and think it was him who got her pregnant. That plan did not work, so he abused his power as the king and eventually had an innocent man murdered. His sexual sin led him into a series of sinful acts to cover up what he had done. When the prophet Nathan exposed his sin to him, David repented of it. And his primary confession is recorded for us here in Psalm 51:4 where we read his heart about his offense. To paraphrase David's words, "My sin is first and foremost an offense against You, God!" David knows he sinned against Uriah and Bathsheba. He realizes he had abused his God-given position as king of Israel. He knows he forced his general to betray one of his soldiers by allowing the enemy to kill him. He is not saying that those people could not accuse him of sinning against them. He is making the point that repentance recognizes that every sin is, first and foremost, a great offense against God.

For our repentance to be complete, that is where we must start. We cannot skip or eliminate this initial step in our change of direction. We must begin by bringing our sins to Him. We need His forgiveness. We need His mercy. It is God who we have committed our sin against. It is He who is most offended with our transgression. It is His help we need. We need His grace and power to overcome and change our sinful hearts which have been giving birth to our sinful behavior. We need His wisdom and plans for replacing our sinful behaviors with righteous ones. God's mercy and grace must be our starting point in change. If we do not include God, our repentance will be short-lived and impotent. We rob ourselves of the power we need to overcome our sins if we leave God out of the process!

Biblical Repentance: Turn, Turn, Turn

If one was to look up the definition of the word *repent,* you would find that the word fundamentally has to do with the concept of movement and direction. It means we have been heading one way and we change our course and go in the opposite direction. To repent means to turn around. I once heard one pastor mistakenly say repentance meant we make a 360 degree turn. In spite of the fact that I knew what he meant, I had to chuckle inside because even though doing a 360 is definitely turning around, if you do a 360, you will end up heading in the same direction! He obviously meant we should do a 180 so that in the end we were heading the opposite direction, not the same one!

The directional change of repentance is a change of heart, a change of mind, and a change of behavior. In repentance, we seek to change that we desire what is sinful. That is not something we want to continue to do. We consciously strive to change the fact that we spend too much time thinking about how to satisfy our sinful desires. And most definitely, we are out to stop doing what we know we should not. Sin has got to go, not only in the outward expression, but also on the inside. In Hebrews 6:1 we come across the idea that repentance is to be about us turning "from acts that lead to death." God has revealed in His Word what is wrong, what is sinful, what is evil, and what is forbidden. As God's Word defines those things that are sinful to us, we are to move in a direction that is away from them. There must be distance placed between us and those things.

But this directional change inherent in repentance is not only a turning away from sin but also a turning toward God. If we are heading in the wrong direction, we certainly must alter our course, but we must alter it in such a way so that we are heading in the right direction! Do you remember the instructions Gideon received in what he was supposed to do about the idols of Baal and Asherah? Gideon was told to break down the altar to Baal, to cut down the Asherah pole, and to build a proper altar to God to replace them. He was told to use the destroyed idols as fuel for the fire when he burned a true and holy sacrifice to the Lord on the new altar. God wanted the idols destroyed but also wanted them replaced.

Repentance is not only turning away from something but also turning toward something else. Yes, God has defined for us what is sinful and wicked, but He has also defined for us what is holy and righteous. Repentance includes replacing what is evil with what is good. Repentance means replacing what is wicked with what is righteous. Repentance is concerned with doing away with sin by doing what is right. Any repentance that does not include the concept of replacing what was sinful with what is holy is merely partial. Repentance is never complete until the appropriate behavior is present in place of the sin which used to be there!

That pastor who said repentance is a 360 degree turnaround made an error of geometrical proportions, but in his error he unknowingly highlighted a regular reality about repentance. If we think repentance only includes turning away from sinful things, we are deficient in our understanding. If we do not replace our sinful behaviors with righteous ones, we will eventually return to the old behavior and in the end our repentance will be a 360 degree turn-around. And we will have missed a big part of Gideon's instructions.

Listen to me, men. If you have turned sex into an idol, you must repent. You must be broken about your sinfulness. You must see your sin as a clear violation of God's commands. First and fore-most, you are sinning against Him! We need His forgiveness. We need His help. We need to tear down the idol and replace it with what is holy and good.

Accessories to Aid with Repentance

In the Scriptures, there are other commands and instructions that can be useful in fleshing out our repentance. These things can be helpful tools for the demolition of our idols. In dealing with sex-ual idolatry, we should be willing to pull out all the stops so that our demolition is totally complete. It might get messy, but get out the sledgehammer, the jackhammer, the crowbars. Hey, bring out the dynamite! Why not? This idol has got to go, so whatever it takes, let's tear it down!

Accessory 1: Confession

Let's start with confession. The word confess literally means "to say the same thing as." This is not the exact idea we have in mind when we think of confession. We usually think that confession means to tell someone else about the wrong things you have done. And it does mean that. But at the core, confession expresses that your heart and mind are in agreement with what God says about something. If God says something is sinful, then you agree. And because you agree, you "say the same thing" about it that God does.

If God says something is sexually immoral, then we are to agree with Him about it. And if that sinful thing is in our hearts and in our lives, we agree that we are guilty of committing that sin. Confession then becomes the process of owning responsibility for that sin, agree-ing that it is sinful and then telling someone else about our trans-gression. We confess to them that we have violated God's command.

We confess to them that God is right when He says that behavior is sinful. We confess that we were doing what He said not to. We confess that it is bad and that we no longer want to do that. We confess that it would be good to be free from that sin. Our confession does not blame someone else for our actions. Confession does not excuse or condone sinful actions we have engaged in because that would not be "saying the same thing as" God.

Have you ever heard someone "confess" a sin by saying something like, "I know what I did was bad, but..."? Whenever we add the word "but" to the end of our confession, we are about to justify or excuse our behavior. And usually, our excuse is built on the premise that someone else is to blame. "I know it's wrong to yell at you, *but* when you act like that it just gets me so mad!" Or in my situation, "I know it was wrong to look at pornography, *but* my wife isn't giving me what I need sexually." When we blame someone else for our sin, we are not saying the same thing as God. God says we are responsible for our own behavior. God tells us to obey Him even if others do not. God says we are not to be overcome by evil but overcome evil with good. God gives us certain instructions on how to behave in response to other sins (i.e., turn the other cheek, love those who hate, bless those who curse, pray for those who persecute you, etc.). Our feelings and what we do with them are ours. Our actions are ours. Our sins are our responsibility. They cannot be blamed on someone else. We must take complete ownership of them.

Adam and Eve established the blame game in the garden of Eden. Adam blamed his sin on Eve (and in a way, the Lord) and Eve blamed her sin on the serpent. They looked for somewhere else to place responsibility for their sin, and they found it! The blame game probably stems from the shame connected with our sin. Shame makes us not want to own responsibility. If we have sinned, in our minds we think that means we are terrible people. We do not want others to think that way about us, and so we want to hide our sin from them, cover them with whatever fig leaves we might be able to find. But if we are to utilize this accessory of confession, we must be able to overcome our shame. There is a humility required to be able to tell someone else that what God has defined as wicked or sinful is present in us. Confession forces humility to be at work in our situation. The Bible tells us, "God resists the proud but gives grace to the humble" (James 4:6). In our desire to repent of our sin, we want God's grace, not His resistance. And humility is the channel which brings His grace to our circumstances. So confess! Even if you must swallow your pride to do it, confess your sins!

Look closely and you will see that confession is the "coming clean" part of godly sorrow that we just looked at. And confession can be a great assistance in repentance. But who should we confess to? When we are dealing with sexual idolatry, should we just confess our sin to anyone and everyone? I do not think so. Here are some guidelines which I am convinced are built on biblical principles here for confessing your sexual idolatry to others:

1. Confession of sin can be limited to the scope of people our sins have specifically impacted. When our sins are against someone directly, they deserve our confession. From my personal example, my sin was immediately against my wife and my vow to her to remain faithful to her alone: until death do us part. Jesus has told us that to look at a woman lustfully is committing adultery in our hearts, and so when I looked lustfully at those women in those videos, I sinned against her. She deserved my confession because my sin was directly against her. All confession of sin should include not only the sin committed (remember, we don't grow and change in fuzzy-land) but also the request that who we have offended would grant us their forgiveness. Other sins which may have a broader impact may require a broader confession. If I sinned publicly, then perhaps a public confession would be appropriate.

2. Confession of our sins to others should be timely. By timely I mean two different things: First, that it should be soon after God has convicted us of our sin. Putting off confession can hinder our repentance. But secondly, I mean we should make our confession in a setting which allows time for a response. Perhaps the offended person has some

questions to ask about our sin. Maybe they need to discuss this with you to be able to understand the situation better. You might need to fill in some details that are missing in their perspective about what God has convicted you of. And they may need some time to process exactly what is happening in your relationship.

When I confessed my sin to my wife, the process of reconciliation took some time. She did not grant me forgiveness immediately because she felt my repentance was missing some key ingredients concerning godly sorrow. And guess what? She was correct! As a couple, we had to revisit my confession a few times over a period of three to four weeks before I was truly broken and repentant where Judi fully granted me her forgiveness. She had to work through some issues and so did I.

As a sidenote to address the concept of repenting and seeking forgiveness, I want to give the "confessor" a bit of advice: be patient. When we seek another person's forgiveness, we are asking them to do something which oftentimes is incredibly difficult. Sometimes the pain of our transgression has created some deep wounds. The damage of our actions might not be something they can just immediately let go of. We know God requires His people to forgive others and that our sin against them puts us in the category of people God wants them to forgive. But it is not a "godly sorrow" perspective to require or demand forgiveness from someone we have offended. The attitude that says "I have repented and therefore you must forgive me immediately" does not convey the attitude we just learned about in our discussion on godly sorrow. Godly sorrow realizes that our sin deserves punishment, not mercy. And if someone does not grant us mercy, we should accept that reality as justice; we are getting what we deserve. Their heart and actions are between them and God. They may need some time to work through their hurt with the Lord in private. Give it to them. And pray that God will help them be able to be merciful like He desires. Be willing to do whatever is necessary to mend that broken relationship even if it means you do not get forgiveness immediately.

3. Confession of sin beyond the immediate person we have offended should be limited to people who meet certain qualifications to assist us in overcoming our sin. In the letter to the Galatian church, Paul said that those who are caught in sin should be helped by those who are spiritual (Galatians 6:1). Very often, sexual idolatry requires some outside assistance in overcoming it. It did for me! Many men who have turned sex into an idol in their hearts will need biblical or pastoral counseling. Pornography and sexual immorality should be confessed to the elders in our church, to a small group of strong Christian men, or to a counselor. As more mature believers, pastors and biblical counselors should be involved with the intent to restore you. Their response to your sin should take your sin seriously and believe there is hope for your restoration. They should find their counsel from the Scriptures and require you to be active in replacing your sin with what is holy and righteous.

Accessory 2: Accountability

Naturally, confessing our sins to someone spiritual who is looking to assist in our restoration creates a certain level of accountability. The fact that we have shared our sin with them makes us aware that they know, and, because they know, a little less likely to turn that way again. It is humiliating to have to share our sin with someone else but that is okay. A little humility goes a long way in overcoming sin, and our sin requires a lot of humility! Do not shrink back from that! The fact that someone else knows can be a great assistance in our sanctification. So look for accountability wherever you can find it. Married men can often find accountability in their wife, provided she can deal well with the situation. Some of us need to go outside of our marriage to find that accountability. If you do, find it wherever you can!

The kind of accountability we are looking for is someone, who is, like we have already said, spiritual and mature in the faith. Someone who knows and believes what God has to say about sex and purity. This person can be someone who has struggled and overcome their own sexual idols, or someone who has kept those idols from finding a place in their own hearts. Sometimes people put restrictions on who they might receive help from, limiting their counselors to others who have dealt with the same problems they are facing. I do not think that limitation is necessary. You may find some common ground with the person who has fallen and gotten back up, and they might be able to help you walk the same path they have had to travel, but walking and not falling might be a better qualification than falling and getting back up. Jesus never fell into temptation, yet He is wonderfully able to help us in our time of need (Hebrews 4:15–16)!

Either way, those who hold us accountable should be able to ask us the difficult questions we need to answer. Questions that are beyond just the typical, "How are you doing?" type of interaction. Questions that honest answers would directly expose any remnant of our idol. Questions that if we do not lie in response to will "hold our feet to the fire" and challenge our purity. Remember how our idols like to hide! Remember how important confronting our sin needs to be. Remember that your heart is desperately wicked and deceitful beyond all things. Remember that the heart is the shrine where our idols are set up and worshipped. Deep and probing questions go far in uncovering what is hidden. Welcome those types of questions and thank God for the person who is willing to ask them!

And finally, be honest. Accountability is not the cure all. No one can be with you every moment of every day. The only way accountability helps is when you are truthful. You can have twenty mature Christian men in your life asking you all the right questions, giving you great advice, quoting all the right verses, and willing to help, but if you reject their help or pull the wool over their eyes, what does that help? Ultimately, your restoration is up to you. Lies will only cause more harm. Rejection of sound biblical instruction will only contribute to your ruin. Personal responsibility is the main ingredient that makes accountability work.

Accessory 3: Radical Amputation

Radical amputation is a pretty odious term! Radical amputation sounds like desperate measures. Radical amputation sounds like it should be the last thing we do in dealing with anything. Like a person who has cancer, the doctors tell them that surgically removing the tumor is only something they would consider as their last resort because it might be dangerous, and they can't promise it will work for sure. But unlike issues we experience in the medical world, Jesus places radical amputation as the *first* response to the sexual idolatry in our lives. The instructions encouraging Radical amputation comes from the Sermon on the Mount:

> You have heard that it was said, "You shall not commit adultery." But I tell you that anyone who looks at a woman lustfully has already committed adultery with her in his heart. If your right eye causes you to stumble, gouge it out and throw it away. It is better for you to lose one part of your body than for your whole body to be thrown into hell. And if your right hand causes you to stumble, cut it off and throw it away. It is better for you to lose one part of your body than for your whole body to go into hell. (Matthew 5:27–30 NIV)

Radical amputation is Jesus's remedy for sexual sin. He is the One who instructed us to deal so drastically with sexual idols. Just as the Lord told Gideon to demolish the idols of Baal and Asherah, Jesus tells you and me to do the same. The heart sin of sexual idolatry is on the chopping block. Adultery is taking place in the heart and expressing itself through physical extremities. And Jesus says this situation should be handled in an extreme way.

Everyone knows Jesus was not being literal here. He did not expect His followers to go get degrees in the medical field so they could become surgeons on themselves. He is not intending His people to walk around half blind and missing appendages. You would be hard-pressed to find anyone who believed Jesus was expecting His disciples to saw off their hands or dig out their eyeballs. However, just because He was not being literal does not mean He was not being radical. When we explain these instructions as Jesus using "shock factor" or hyperbole to impress something upon His disciples, we are in danger of missing His point. Jesus does not want you to take Him literally, but He does expect you to do something crazy about your sin. He expects you to go to extreme measures to rid yourself of sexual idolatry. "Cut of your hand! Gouge out your eye!" Jesus is saying that you need to see this situation from God's point of view! Your sexual sin could have eternal consequences! Take this thing seriously as if your life depended on it…because it does!

What does radical amputation look like in the life of someone dealing with sexual idolatry? It looks like us cutting off things in our life that promote and encourage sexual immorality. Think of all the things that contribute to your sexual idolatry. A couple of things come to mind immediately: pornography or movies with sex scenes. What does Jesus want you to do with those things? I think the answer is obvious. *He wants you to go through the process of making it impossible for those things to lead you into sexual sin ever again.* If you gouged out your eye and threw it away, that eye could never be used by you again. Ever. Same thing with your hand. If you cut off your hand and threw it in the trash, you will have lost the use of that appendage forever. In order for you to apply this instruction to your situation, you need to look for ways to make it impossible for the things which contributed to your sexual sin from ever doing it again.

Take the question to the next level. How do you make it so pornography or sexually explicit movies can never feed your sexual idolatry again? (This is where people find it difficult to put Jesus's words into practice!) Those things come into our lives through our internet and computer and television…sometimes our smartphones and tablets and laptops. They find entry into our lives through entertainment. They find channels into our hearts during our downtime and veg out moments. Sex in our society is embedded in so many places that it may be nearly impossible to root out every little thing that feeds our sexual idolatry. But the things we can, we must!

Unfortunately, this is where the objections begin to surface! You might be thinking some of them now. Maybe you have heard them. They sound like this: "I need my computer! How am I supposed to do my work without it?" Or maybe it sounds something like "I cannot punish my family for my sin by removing the TV from my home." How about "Man, I've just got to have a cell phone!" or "If we don't have the internet, we'll be stuck in the Stone Age!" So many arguments and objections to how Jesus's instructions could be lived out in their life. Believe me, you are not the only person who has to wrestle with the implications and complications of Jesus's instructions. These objections and more have been uttered in our "modern-day" response to Jesus's primitive commands. "Jesus doesn't really expect that from me, does He?"

The serious disciple of Jesus needs to come to grips with this reality. He does expect that of you.

Jesus does expect you to take this thing extremely serious! If He did not expect it of you, He would not have said what He said! I have a hard time imagining getting to heaven and Jesus pulling us aside to tell us, "Hey, I was just exaggerating about that radical amputation thing. I did not really want you to go to extremes in dealing with your sexual immorality. You misunderstood me. Sorry about that. I should have been clearer."

What is ironic about these objections is that people know and understand the clear application of Jesus's command in their life. They know their laptop is the "right eye" of Jesus's illustration. They understand that the internet or smartphone is the "right hand" causing them to stumble. Just ask someone struggling with a sexual idol what causes them to stumble. They know the answer! The problem is they see how hard cutting off those things will be for them. Implementing Jesus's instructions in their situation will inconvenience them. Life will quickly become extremely difficult or limited for them. It will be like being half blind or missing a hand! Really? Go figure! They see what needs to go and yet hope for a different solution. Many men talk themselves into trying a different approach first to see if something else will work. In effect, they are opting for the "surgery is the last option" mentality, all the while missing the point that Jesus is saying, "Surgery is the only option!"

That means we must come up with ways to rid those things from our lives. We install the necessary software, we switch our phones to flip phones, we cancel cable and Netflix. We take measures to rob ourselves of the privacy associated with our laptops and computers by putting them in open areas where anyone could see them at any time. We agree to not use electronics after our wife has gone to sleep. We choose movies that not only are void of sex scenes but also free from anything sexually inappropriate.

Wait a minute! I can hear it now... "You mean I only get to watch cheesy Christian movies?" I was not totally saying that but hey, why not? What is the matter with paying the price of cheesy Christian movies for sexual purity? I know from experience that the cheesy Christian movie industry is getting less and less cheesy.

And movies are not the only form of entertainment we need to be on guard against containing things that feed our sexual idols. Some video games, certain books, even commercials during sporting events can be a problem for some of us. For some men, working out at the gym can present us with the temptation to look lustfully at a woman. What are we to do about it? Find a different place or time to work out! Cut off the eye or hand that makes us stumble. Do not go to the public pool if it is too much of an issue for you. Do not watch the girls beach volleyball tournament if there is temptation there. Whatever you do, do not shy away from whatever radical step you must take to remove the idol!

One of the ways sexual immorality found its way into my life was through Facebook and Instagram. For some odd reason, once I turned fifty years old, Facebook began posting ads on my wall that had to do with erectile dysfunction. Apparently, they assumed I had the same struggle other men of my advanced years have in that department. Very often those ads are nothing more than hidden links to small clips with pornographic content. Those ads were a temptation for me. Instagram also had various paths through hashtags that could bring me to pornographic clips as well. Because those apps were temptations to sin, they quickly found themselves in the trash bin on my laptop and cell phone.

Do not make the mistake of thinking that we only need to amputate the obvious things that people would recognize as fuel for sexual idolatry. Sure, pornography and sexually explicit entertainment should go. However, different things contain different temptations for each of us. Some are big and obvious; some are small and disguised. More than anyone else, you are the one who knows what little temptations feed your idol. Those things have got to go as well.

There are many steps we can take to gouge out the eye and cut off the hand. We must resist the urge to give in to the "It's going to be hard" response. In obedience to Jesus, we deal with the inconveniences missing a hand or an eye creates for us. We have got to take this just as seriously as He does.

Flee Sexual Immorality

The Bible is littered with commands that highlight the reality that sexual sin needs to be dealt with in radical ways. Look at a couple more with me:

> Flee sexual immorality! (1 Corinthians 6:18 NIV)

What does this mean? When it comes to sexual sins, you must get as far away as fast as you can! You do not play with it. You do not hang around it. You do not stay close to sexual temptations. Like Joseph, you run out of the room when immorality is trying to get its hands on you, leaving your coat behind if necessary!

Here is another one:

> But among you there must not be even a hint of sexual immorality. (Ephesians 5:3 NIV)

You know what a hint is, right? A hint is just a small suggestion, a little bit of flavor present in the dish, like someone saying,

"I can taste a just hint of garlic in this." Or if someone is trying to solve a riddle and they ask for a hint. They are saying, "Just tell me something that helps point me in the right direction or clues me in to just a small part of the answer." Not even having a hint of sexual immorality among us means we have done the work of removing any "flavor" of sexual sin from our lives, even the smallest amount.

That sounds radical to me!

Once I was traveling down the interstate and saw a billboard that read, "What part of 'Thou shalt not' don't you understand?" I laughed inside a bit at the clever way someone had chosen to sum up the commandments. This was at a time when Christians were renting signs and putting "messages from God" all over the place. A quick Google search revealed that some were pretty clever and some, not so much. In my search I came across another one that read, "That love your neighbor thing...I meant it." Those "God billboards" were interesting ways of getting people to think about God, but these two specifically highlight something about us that needs to be made clear: *we need to stop thinking that obeying God is optional!* The Bible was not written just so we would know stuff. The Bible was breathed out by God in order to bring us liberty and freedom, to lead us in ways that brought blessing and benefit to our lives. The key to that equation is found in doing what God says! Like James told us,

> But be doers of the word, and not hearers only, deceiving yourselves. He who looks into the perfect law of liberty and continues in it, and is not a forgetful hearer but a doer of the work, this one will be blessed in what he does. (James 1:22, 25 NKJV)

God has communicated how serious He is about our idolatry. Demolishing the idol is our only remedy. Tearing it down and throwing it in the fire is the God-honoring thing to do. Cutting it off so it can never grow back again is how Jesus expects His followers to handle sexual idols. Let's be doers of the Word and discover the blessing doers experience!

CHAPTER 7

GETTING YOUR HEART RIGHT

Here O Israel, the Lord our God, the Lord is One. And you
shall love the Lord your God with all your heart, with all
your soul, with all your mind and with all your strength.
—Mark 12:29–30 NKJV

Anyone who has ever taken on a renovation project knows that
the project gets finished in phases. Repentance is the demolition
phase. However, demolition is only the first step in finishing the
project. When that phase is complete, the job is only partially
done. Once our sexual idol has been revealed and demolished, we
have much more work to accomplish. Never make the mistake
of thinking that the job is complete just because we have done
everything we read about in the last chapter. Beyond a shadow
of a doubt, the devil hates it when we repent. But if he can convince you that repentance was enough, he is confident he can get
his idol back on the throne of your heart. Consider these words
of Jesus and see if they have any application to the issue we are
addressing:

> When an impure spirit comes out of a per-
> son, it goes through arid places seeking rest and
> does not find it. Then it says, "I will return to
> the house I left." When it arrives, it finds the

house swept clean and put in order. Then it goes and takes seven other spirits more wicked than itself, and they go in and live there. And the final condition of that person is worse than the first. (Matthew 12:43–45 NIV)

The devil is out for your destruction; he always has been. He really loves that last sentence of Jesus's teaching here: "The final condition of that person is worse than the first." He views your life as a "renovation project" too, but his plan is to wreck the house, not to make home improvements! And he just might see your repentance as a momentary inconvenient setback in accomplishing his ultimate plan for your life, which is: "to steal, to kill and to destroy" (John 10:10). If you have accomplished the "demolition phase" of repentance, he plans to return to see if you have finished renovating. Have you done *all of the work* God requires, beyond just demolition? It is imperative that you realize that your repentance places you at a crucial moment in your sanctification. Do not stop there. Just like in the story of Gideon, God is looking for a proper altar in your heart where holy and acceptable sacrifices are made.

New Year's resolutions are usually a good example of this reality. Most people who make New Year's resolutions, within a month or two have already returned to whatever bad habit they were out to remedy. Many do not even last that long. And while those types of resolutions usually are not as important as the topic we are talking about, human nature can be the same in both situations. Solomon also noticed this dynamic in the typical approach to turning over a new leaf as we read what he wrote in Proverbs:

As a dog returns to his own vomit, so a fool repeats his folly. (Proverbs 26:11 NKJV)

None of us wants to be thought of as a fool, so let's get to the process of rebuilding a proper altar and develop a God-pleasing perspective on sex.

Shema: God First

On one occasion when Jesus was dealing with the scheming
Scribes and Pharisees, they decided to test Him by giving Him some
difficult theological riddles which they hoped would trip Him up.
They wanted to find something in His response which would make
Him look bad in the eyes of the huge crowds which had grown to
respect Him. Jesus knew their intent was to trap Him, and yet He
answered them openly and soundly. Those guys would never learn
their lesson that Jesus was infinitely superior to them in every way!
There were many who were witnesses to this entire exchange, and
one of them was a teacher of the law. When he noticed that Jesus
had put them in their place with sound theological explanations, he
decided to ask another question, one he seemed genuinely interested
to know what the answer was. He said to Jesus, "Teacher, what is the
most important commandment God has ever given us to obey?" In
other words, "If people who were interested in pleasing God wanted
to give their attention to what God thought was most important,
which command would help them do that?"

In His response, Jesus quoted what is known in Jewish circles as
"the Shema." "Hear O Israel, the Lord your God, the Lord is One.
You shall love the Lord your God with all of your heart, with all of
your soul, with all of your mind and with all of your strength." These
words which are the starting point for many Jewish prayers are called
the Shema because the first word translated "hear" comes from the
Hebrew word "sh'ma."

In examining His response, many people want to jump right
into the part about loving the Lord with all your heart, soul, mind,
and strength. Some of us might even want to get to the second part
of His answer, which was "Love your neighbor as yourself." Jesus
taught us that all the rest of the commands of God get their significance from these two commands. However, I want to pause a
moment with the first part of the Shema to see if there might be
something that gets overlooked by moving on too quickly into the
other parts of Jesus's answer.

When we discussed the command against idolatry and what idolatry was at its essence, we discovered that the heart of idolatry is built on the concept that we would look to something other than God to provide something that only He can. God presents Himself as being the Sufficient One, the Sole Provider for our lives. However, a fallen perspective can lead us to think a thing or a person or some situation can give us what God alone can provide. As fallen men we can believe that any number of "created things" could provide us with fulfillment, worth, purpose, or meaning. But Jesus says, "The Lord our God is One." I am not foolish enough to miss the possibility that this statement has multiple applications for our lives, but one of the things it *certainly* means is that the Lord is the only One who we should view as God. The Lord is the Primary, the Only, the Singular, the Exclusive. There is none other who we should worship or serve.

What is the best way I can say this? If there is anything else in our hearts or lives that vies for the position that God alone deserves, *we are in danger of violating the most important commandment.* And not only that. If we are off on this commandment, then all the rest of our lives are also in danger of being out of whack. Remember, Jesus told the teacher of the law who asked Him this question that the rest of the instructions God has given us hangs on us getting the primary one right! There is no other command more important!

When we tear down the idol which we have made of sex, it creates a space that needs to be filled. That space creates a vacuum which unless we purposefully deal with it, something will move into its slot. We might make a similar mistake people trying to overcome addictions make when they replace their addiction with another created thing. For instance, people who are addicted to alcohol or drugs might replace it with a "healthy alternative" like running or lifting weights. For the Christian, what Jesus said about the Lord our God being the "One" thing in our life should give us the alternative for the vacuum created by the destruction of our idol. Jesus Himself needs to be moved on to the altar in our heart!

Jesus is what should replace the idol we have destroyed. Our need is to love the Lord more than anything. He must be on the throne, and our love for Him must be what moves Him there. With all our heart, soul, mind, and strength, we must build that altar in our heart *for Him*. We have to see Jesus as everything to us and for us. This is the first place to start in replacing our sexual idol. If we do not start there, nothing else we do will be effective in preventing this idol, or others, from taking up residence there. Hear, O Israel! The Lord is One. You shall love the Lord Your God with all your heart, with all your soul, with all your mind and all your strength.

Renewing Our Mind

Establishing God as central in our lives is the starting place for replacing sexual idolatry, but there is more that must be done. The perspectives about sex which the world has implanted in our minds must be deleted (to steal an analogy from the computer world) and replaced with the proper programming. We must install the right software and then reboot the system! That process is what the Bible calls "renewing our minds." Notice Paul's instructions to the Church in Ephesus.

> But you have not so learned Christ, if indeed you have heard Him and have been taught by Him, as the truth is in Jesus: that you put off, concerning your former conduct, the old man which grows corrupt according to the deceitful lusts, and be renewed in the spirit of your mind, and that you put on the new man which was created according to God, in true righteousness and holiness. (Ephesians 4:20–24 NKJV)

Paul's instructions are essential for you at this point in the renovation project. He first says that there is a certain way we "learn Christ." How we grow in our relationship with Him or being "taught by Him" happens through a threefold process. If you want to get to know and love Jesus better, this is how it happens: First, put off the old man. That is the demolition process which we have already discussed. The second and third phases (being renewed in the spirit of your mind and putting on the new man) are what we are discussing presently. Being renewed in our minds is the reprogramming which God's Word does to our thoughts and perspectives about sex. The way this works is by saturating our minds with what the Bible teaches. We need to read, study, be taught, read some more, and study some more until we really get it. The end goal is that we eventually think biblically about sex.

If you are a Christian, you should value what God thinks about things. You should also know that the only place we find out what God thinks about things is in His Word. And trust me, God's Word is not silent about sex. It may come as a surprise for some of you to realize that God has a lot to say about it! He invented sex, and because He invented sex, He knows what it is all about. To develop a perspective on sex without His input would be the epitome of foolishness.

To get you started thinking right about sex, here are a few fundamental things God's Word teaches us about it.

First: sex is good. This may be a difficult reality for some people to accept. There are many ways which we might develop the thought that sex is a bad thing. So many of our ideas concerning sex come from the selfish approach most people bring to it, both ourselves and others. Desires that God has placed in each of us have been tainted by our sinful nature and perverted into using sex as a selfish opportunity to sin. Because that dynamic is prevalent in so many people, we conclude that sex itself is sinful. Our verdict is based on the premise of "guilt by association." Our experience with our own sexual sin, as well as the sinful expressions of others, may cause us to think of sex as a necessary evil. Necessary because of the need to procreate, but evil nonetheless. However, that is not what the Bible teaches.

In the beginning, God created sex.

> So God created man in His own image;
> in the image of God He created him; male and
> female He created them. (Genesis 1:27 NKJV)

When God formed Adam from the dust of the earth, He shaped Him with His reproductive organs as a part of His body. All of it: the organs, the glands, the hormones...everything! Same with Eve. When God took Adam's rib and fashioned it into the first woman, He created Her with each of her reproductive organs in place. Also, He planned how male and female organs would function together with their spouses in all aspects of who we are sexually. He made it like that in order to create the melodic symphony which making love ought to bring to a marriage.

Not only did God fashion the physical aspects needed for a husband and wife to engage in sexual intercourse; He also blessed the activity!

> Then God blessed them, and God said to
> them, "Be fruitful and multiply." (Genesis 1:28
> NKJV)

If you ask the average person what the first commandment was that God gave to Adam and Eve, they will probably tell you He told them not to eat from the tree of knowledge. The forbidden fruit is what many people (even Christians) would give as their final answer. They would be wrong. God's first command to Adam and Eve was to be fruitful and multiply. I know you realize this but let me just say it. In order for them to obey God's command, they were required to have sex! There was no other way for Adam and Eve to be fruitful and multiply without it.

For those who do not study their Bibles closely, allow me to point out the obvious: this command to be fruitful and multiply is in chapter 1 of Genesis. That command is given on day six of the Creation account. This is *prior to* chapter 3 when Adam and Eve disobeyed God and brought sin into the world. God formed Adam and Eve with the physical capabilities to enjoy and engage in sex and then blessed their sexuality with the command to procreate! In light of this information, the logical conclusion we should come to is that sex is good...or as God says a few verses later, "it was very good!" (Genesis 1:31).

All the perversions and sins which fallen humanity have committed in their misuse of sex cannot change this reality. God created sex and sex is "very good."

Second: sex is to be limited to marriage. While it is true that God created sex and that sex is good, we cannot ignore the fact that sex has been given boundaries. In various places, God's Word goes into specific details in order to define what is God honoring and appropriate for men sexually. I am not going to spend the time necessary to cover every commandment given regarding man's sexual activity, but I do want to highlight the main one. Sex was created by God and sanctioned for only a certain segment of the population: a man and woman who have covenanted together in the sacred bonds of holy matrimony! Human sexuality has been purposefully limited by God to take place in the confines of a committed lifelong relationship between a husband and his wife. There is no other situation where sexual activity is pleasing to God. His intent from the beginning was that only married couples would have sex.

This communicates a couple things to us married couples. The first is this: if God created sex and thinks it is "very good," then God is pleased when married couples enjoy sex free from idolatry! It makes God happy when married couples experience the full joy sex is intended to bring to the marriage bed. Here is a shocking revelation to many Christian husbands: *we can please God by having sex with our wife*! There are many ways we please God in our activities and behaviors, and sex in marriage is just one of them...but do not miss this truth: idolatry-free sex in marriage brings a smile to God's face. We can rejoice in knowing that it is God honoring for us to enjoy having sex with our wife!

The second thing this tells us is that husbands should focus their sexual thoughts and energies entirely on their wife. There is no other person in the whole world we are permitted to have sex with. There is no other person in the world we should even think that way about. None. Do not forget Jesus's instruction about committing adultery in the heart by thinking lustfully about another woman. That teaching should limit you. It should guide you. It should help you focus on the only woman in the world that God has approved for you.

When sex is an idol to us, it creates some troublesome dynamics in our marriages. The sexual element of our marriage gets compared to image of sex which we "worship" (i.e., does she have the right physical attributes, does she value sex as highly as me, does she react in sexual situations like she is supposed to, etc.?). As husbands, you and I should not be in the business of comparing our wife with others. She should not be forced to be someone other than the woman God has created her to be. The command to not covet our neighbor's wife comes to mind here. Your wife is not your neighbor's wife, and your neighbor's wife is not yours. Comparing and contrasting is never to be present in your sexual relationship with your wife!

Your wife is a unique person. There is no one else on the planet that is specifically identical to her...or you for that matter. When you join two unique individuals in marriage, you inevitably create a unique relationship. No other marriage on earth will be exactly the same as yours. Your wife is different than any other woman. This means she will have strengths and weaknesses and attributes which will contribute to your marriage to make it unique. It is wrong for you to think the sexual aspect of your marriage will be just like some image you have created in your mind, whether that image was created by past experiences, movies, books, or pornography. It should be what the two of you together create it to be—nothing more, nothing less.

The ingredients which we bring to our bedrooms combine into a recipe unique to every marriage. Those flavors are for husbands and wives to discover and enjoy together. Physical attractiveness, hormones, frequency of sexual encounters, what turns her off and what turns her on...those are things which you cannot predetermine for your wife. Those are the things you need to learn about her. Those are things you must accept about her and give your attention to. Your focus cannot be somewhere else, or you will miss out on the uniqueness of sex in your own marriage. Your wife has her own attributes that contribute to her overall beauty and attractiveness, and it is your job as her husband to focus on her beauty and hers alone!

This could mean that you need to reprogram your mind based on what God thinks is beautiful. Beauty may not be what the world around you says it is. I know this will sound cliché, but beauty that is merely external is not true beauty. True beauty, from God's perspective, goes far beyond something physical. As a Christian man, your concept of what ingredients combine to make a woman beautiful must be based on what God's Word says, not on what the culture has programmed you to think. Read with me what God would have us to understand about the true nature of beauty found both here in 1 Peter 3:2–5 and in Proverbs 31:30:

> When they see the purity and reverence of your lives. Your beauty should not come from outward adornment, such as elaborate hairstyles and the wearing of gold jewelry or fine clothes. Rather, it should be that of your inner self, the unfading beauty of a gentle and quiet spirit, which is of great worth in God's sight. For this is the way the holy women of the past who put their hope in God used to adorn themselves. (1 Peter 3:2–5 NIV)

And the summation of almost an entire chapter on what a wonderful wife is all about:

> Charm is deceptive, and beauty is fleeting;
> but a woman who fears the LORD is to be praised.
> (Proverbs 31:30 NIV)

From these verses we can see clearly that beauty is much more than just something you can see with your eyes. God wants Christian husbands to think beauty includes greater attributes than hair and lips and shapely bodies. He expects you to be impressed by deeper things than hairstyles and clothing and jewelry. Purity and reverence and a submissive spirit combine to form true beauty in a woman. Her inner strength which flows from a gentle and quiet spirit and a heart that fears the Lord are to be the highest attributes of beauty which Christian men value. Your wife's beauty comes from more than just her curves. Pretty hair and makeup and fancy clothes can lead us away from what makes a woman truly beautiful, and we should not allow the world to deceive us like that.

Search for the beauty which is in your wife. She has a beauty that is all her own. Do not compare her with others or with the world's standard of beauty. Do not think that what you saw in a magazine or a movie is what you should find in her. Learn to appreciate her own unique attributes: her strengths and even her weaknesses. You will be glad you did! For you, it must be all about her and no one else.

The limits on sex are put there intentionally by God. He is a loving God and everything He does contains some element of love in it. Those who do not know God think that the limits He placed on sex are cruel and "unloving." They seem to grasp the notion that God made something incredibly wonderful when He invented sex, but then for some reason, they imagine it an act of cruelty to limit a man to sex with just one woman for an entire lifetime. They imagine God as a sadistic deity who wants to torment His creation by robbing them of a great pleasure. The devil's words to Eve in the garden resonated with the same accusation, that God's limitation prevented them from experiencing something wonderful. But this accusation is baseless, and the numbers reveal that God's plan is ultimately the better one in the end. Statistics show that monogamous married couples are happier, healthier, live longer, have sex more often, and have more satisfying sex than single people.[18] Surprise, surprise!

Third: God had purposes behind creating sex. In the process of renewing our minds about sex, we need to understand, at least in a small sense, the reasons behind God creating sex. My counselor had me study this during our time together in order to help renew my own mind about God's purposes behind inventing sex.[19] Because He is a purposeful Creator, God does nothing without a reason. When

---

[18] Mark Gungor, *Laugh Your Way to a Better Marriage.*
[19] Lee Edmonds, *Marriage and Intimacy.*

He invented sex, He had specific purposes in mind. In His Word, we find those purposes spelled out. Let's examine a few of them.

1.   Reproduction

In the initial command associated with sex, we see one of the purposes behind God inventing sex was for mankind to be fruitful and multiply. God desires humans to not only be productive but reproductive as well! He wants us to fill the earth and exercise dominion over it. When Noah and his family came out of the ark, God voiced the same desire again, "Be fruitful and multiply" (Genesis 9:1). In the book of Malachi, when God was highlighting that His people were violating their marriage covenant through divorce and mistreatment of their wives, He let them know that one of His purposes behind marriage was that they would produce godly offspring (Malachi 2:13–16). David tells us in the Psalms that children are an inheritance from the Lord. They are like arrows in the hands of a warrior and the man with a full quiver is blessed by God (Psalm 127:3–5).

God loves children and He desires to see godly marriages produce godly families which help create godly societies. Godly societies bring the blessings of God on entire nations. Sexual activity in marriage is the fundamental ingredient in that process that gets that ball rolling. From the beginning, reproduction has been one of the purposes behind sex.

2.   Developing intimacy between husband and wife

God is not only interested in married couples making babies. He has other purposes in mind behind sex. In Genesis 2 where we find the more detailed account of God creating Adam and Eve, we hear God declare another one of His purposes behind the invention of sex: two becoming one. He says,

> Therefore shall a man leave his father and
> his mother and shall cleave unto his wife: and
> they shall be one flesh. (Genesis 2:24 KJV)

Two separate people becoming one with each other. This speaks of an intimate act in marriage which no other relationship is intended to experience. Sex is intended to create intimacy and oneness for you and your wife.

When a man enters marriage, he is one person with his own unique personality and perspective. He marries another unique individual that he must now get to know and love. Developing love and intimacy includes potential problems and pitfalls. It is always the closest relationships which create the situations where we are most vulnerable to be hurt. The closer we get to someone else, the more vulnerable we become. It is a catch-22, but for a husband and wife to develop intimacy, they must expose themselves to one another— make themselves vulnerable.

God is aware of this principle in relationships, but He knows that the equation which produces intimacy does not work without vulnerability! Without vulnerability we cannot achieve love and intimacy. Without it we cannot learn what it is to trust. Without placing ourselves at risk, we cannot know the depths of "oneness" which we can experience in marriage. But obviously, God thinks it is worth the risk. The risk of being hurt is worth the reward of deep intimacy in marriage!

There are many areas in marriage where we experience "getting to know" one another. Sex is one of them. Clearly when we make love, we have the physical reality of exposing ourselves to our spouse. It is impossible to have sex with your clothes on. Certain areas of our bodies must be exposed in order for sex to happen! Being naked with your spouse includes many emotional variables. When the clothes come off, what is hidden becomes visible. In that situation we are faced with certain difficulties to work through, questions that run through our minds. Can I trust them enough to expose myself to them? Am I attractive to them? Is there anything about me which disappoints them? Answers to questions like those are often found in the way our spouse responds to us sexually. And believe me, this is a delicate matter! Both men and women can have strong sensitivities in this area of feeling like they are good enough for their spouse.

Making love also includes the concept of being concerned with what is pleasing to our spouse. Sex presents us with the opportunity to both give and receive pleasure from our mate. This giving and receiving mostly begins outside of the bedroom but then culminates in the way we interact with each other in bed. Sex was never intended to be one-sided, where just one of us enjoys it. Like the rest of our marriage, sex works best when there is giving and receiving. In our beds, we must learn what pleases our spouse and give our attention to that. When the husband and wife are working together, sex strengthens our marriages. When we are not, it can have the opposite effect.

In order to work together well, we must be able to communicate. For good sex there must be good communication. This communication could be verbal or nonverbal (or both), but it must happen. In this way, sex is a microcosm of the entire relationship. Poor communication in our relationship reveals itself in the bedroom. This can be a catalyst for working on communication issues in other areas of the marriage, especially if couples know it will improve things in the bedroom! For both husband and wife, sex presents the opportunity to work together and strengthen many different aspects of their relationship.

Clearly, God designed sex so it would enhance our marriages. It was a brilliant idea on His part! Sex gives us the opportunity to express our love for one another, to enjoy our spouse and be enjoyed by them. Sex can also reveal problem areas in our relationship that need to improve, and it can give us the opportunity to work on those problems! The act of making love is a process which draws husbands and wives together as they work together to do it well. That development of intimacy was one of the main purposes behind God inventing it!

3. Pleasure

I saved the obvious one for last. God invented sex in order to provide married couples with one of the most physically gratifying events a man or woman could ever encounter. Words cannot even express the physical gratification a human body experiences in sexual fulfillment. Poets and musicians have penned words endlessly in order to try to describe feelings that are indescribable. And they will continue to make those attempts throughout human history because sex is so physically wonderful. That is the way God made it!

There can be no doubt that God intended sex to be filled with pleasure. A biological examination of the sexual aspects of the human body alone will indicate clearly to us that we were specifically designed by God to experience great pleasure when we engage in sexual activity. The location of our nerves, the hormones sex releases in us, the rushing of blood to certain parts of our bodies, the excitement which courses through our emotions and thoughts, and the overwhelming feeling of bliss and satisfaction when a man or woman experience an orgasm...all of this and more combine to let us know that sex is intended to be filled with pleasure. How it all works together, biologically speaking, is a miraculous wonder. We can join with David in praising God because we are "fearfully and wonderfully made" (Psalm 139:14)!

A biological study is not the only way we can conclude that God intended sex to be filled with pleasure. When we examine the Scriptures, we find an entire book of the Bible written to celebrate the pleasures associated with sex and marriage. Solomon and his bride go into great poetic detail concerning the joys and pleasures associated with idolatry-free sex in marriage. Here are a few selections from his rapturous writings (try not to forget this is the Bible we are reading here!):

> Let him kiss me with the kisses of his mouth—for your love is better than wine... Draw me away! A bundle of myrrh is my beloved to me, that lies all night between my breasts. (1:2, 4)

> Like an apple tree among the trees of the woods... I sat down in his shade with great delight and his fruit was sweet to my taste. His left hand is under my head and his right hands embraces me. (2:3, 6)

My beloved put his hand by the latch of the door, and my heart yearned for him. I arose to open for my beloved and my hands dripped with myrrh, my fingers with liquid myrrh on the handles of the lock. (5:4–5)

How beautiful are your feet in sandals O prince's daughter! The curves of your thighs are like jewels, the works of the hands of a skillful workman. Your navel is a rounded goblet; it lacks no blended beverage. Your waist is a heap of wheat set about with lilies. Your two breasts are like two fawns, twins of a gazelle. How fair and how pleasant you are, O Love with your delights! This stature of yours is like a palm tree and your breasts like its clusters. I said, "I will go up to the palm tree. I will take hold of its branches." Let now your breasts be like clusters of the vine. (7:1–3, 6–8 all verses NIV)

Many find it hard to believe that verses like this are recorded in the Scriptures, but there they are, expounding on the pleasures and joys of idolatry-free sexual experience in the marriage of the Lover and his Beloved! Recorded in the heart of the Scriptures in Song of Solomon, we have clear biblical verification that God designed sex for husbands and wives to deeply relish in the pleasures it can bring!

Renewing the Mind Continued

Those are some of the reasons God invented sex. And I would testify that those are some pretty great reasons! My marriage has been extremely blessed since I have repented and turned away from my own sexual idolatry. The frustrations and disappointments I used to feel have been replaced with love and affection and intimacy for my wife. Even though we are past the time in our lives of having children (we had a pretty full quiver with nine of them), we certainly have experienced the reality of sex creating a deeper intimacy in our relationship. We have been communicating better and allowing our sexual intimacy to reveal areas in our relationship which we need to improve. When that happens, we roll with it! If there is work that needs to be done, then by all means, let's do it! And finally, I feel compelled to tell you that since Jesus tore down that idol, we have never enjoyed the pleasures of sex more. My previous sexual idolatry had the effect of preventing my wife from fully opening herself up to all that sex could bring to our relationship. Something inside her told her my perspectives about sex were inappropriate. When that idol came down, it did away with her hesitation to engage in "idol worship" with me. I am so thankful for God commanding the altar to be destroyed and the idols to be torn down!

These truths are not only true for me and Judi. Let these realities really sink into your own minds to help develop a God-honoring perspective for you too. And do not simply think that just reading these things once here is sufficient to completely renew your mind. You used to think often about sex through the lens of your idolatry. Now as often as you think about sex, you must do so through the lens of the Scriptures. God's perspective must continually be your perspective. Also, it should go without saying (but I am going to say it anyway), this chapter concerning what the Bible teaches about sex is not an exhaustive study on the matter. You must prayerfully search the Word yourself to receive all God has to say for you and your wife about idolatry-free sex for your marriage. What I have written here are some of the fundamental truths to help get you heading in the right direction of renewing your thoughts which once were governed by an idol.

Just Thinking…

As we can see from what Jesus teaches us, that serpent of old desires to rebuild a sexual idol and enshrine it on the altar of your heart. He wants to destroy and ruin the work which has started regarding your sex life. But we know that God desires to bless your marriage with sex that is holy in His sight. He wants your sex to be something that develops true intimacy and pleasure for you and your wife. Jesus does not want your physical intimacy to be a cheap imitation of the rotten fruit the world tempts us with. Do not settle for anything less than God's best!

Having said that, there is one more element to renewing the mind which I feel compelled to highlight before moving on. One of the main ways I had been deceived concerning thoughts was by believing the lie that said, "That's all they are, just thoughts! They were not really that important. Just thinking is not sinful." I do not mean that I had permitted myself to think about sexually inappropriate things (though some men might). There is no doubt that certain thoughts in my mind were unacceptable. I would not consciously engage in thoughts that might readily be defined as sexually immoral. However, as long as I wasn't thinking "pornographic" thoughts, or "lustful" thoughts about other women, I was convinced my thoughts were not that significant. I was so wrong!

As I look back on things, I find it silly that I had correctly categorized thoughts that were pornographic or lustful as sinful thoughts but had failed to think that sinful thoughts might include more than just those two categories! In hindsight, I am ashamed to admit how silly I was to miss this crucial reality. Every thought we think is important! Every thought we think has a positive or negative impact on who we are spiritually. Every thought we think has the potential to strengthen our relationship with the Lord or weaken it. Every thought we allow to hang out in our brain is a plant we water and fertilize. If it is a right thought, we nourish righteousness in our mind. If it is a wrong thought, we nourish what is wrong in our mind. And (here's the important thing) wrong thoughts about sex are not limited to pornography and lust.

Notice how the apostle Paul spells this out in his second letter to the church in Corinth:

> For though we live in the world, we do not
> wage war as the world does. The weapons we
> fight with are not the weapons of the world. On
> the contrary, they have divine power to demolish

strongholds. We demolish arguments and every pretension that sets itself up against the knowledge of God, and we take captive every thought to make it obedient to Christ. (2 Corinthians 10:3–5 NIV)

The war we are in requires weapons in order for us to win our battles. The weapons which God has provided us are mighty! They are able to pull down this stronghold, this idol which has been set up in our hearts. But our weapon is not a worldly or fleshly weapon. Our weapon has to do with the arguments and thoughts bouncing around in our brains! The weapon he is talking about that is so mighty and effective against strongholds is our ability to properly handle our thoughts!

Do you see what Paul brings up as it pertains to our thoughts? He says they can be arguments and pretentions set up against what God says about things. Our thoughts can be out of line with Him, meaning, His perspective and our perspective are not the same. What happens when our perspective is not the same with someone else? We argue with them. We support our own ideas while degrading the position of our opponent. Our thoughts do that to God! What does it mean if our perspective is not in line with God's? It means we have placed way too much value on our thoughts! We have begun to think too highly of our ideas. That is exactly what pretention is. It is the development of a false notion of importance or worth. When our minds hold a perspective in opposition to what God says, we have exaggerated the value of that perspective. For a simple brain like mine, that means we think something is more important than it actually is.

Wow, that hits home for me! The way I had turned sex into an idol was exactly that: pretention. I had been deceived into thinking my specific image of what constituted good sex was worth everything to me. I had placed such a high value on it that it had the power in my mind to determine if I was fulfilled or not. I had given it the authority to judge if I was a man or not. I had empowered my concept of "good sex" to determine if my wife loved me based on if she acted a certain way sexually. I had exaggerated the importance of sex to such a degree that it began to rob me of my ability to love my wife like Christ loves the church. Talk about a false notion of importance or worth. Sex had moved to idol status in my thoughts. This was far beyond just pornographic or lustful thoughts. These were thoughts that associated my very worth and purpose with sex. These were thoughts that judged my wife's integrity and commitment to her husband based on my own sexual misconceptions. These were thoughts that transferred the qualities of what kind of man I was from who I was in Christ to who I was in bed. Sex was given way too much power in my mind on account of its perceived elevated worth. Pretention almost seems like too kind a word!

Now look at what Paul says we are supposed to do with such thoughts. Take captive every thought and make it obedient to Jesus! The more we renew our minds with the cleansing Word of God, the more we begin to recognize thoughts that are not "obedient to Christ." Recognizing wayward thoughts is a necessary step in the process of renewing our minds. But handling wayward thoughts properly is where the real fighting is done, where the battle is won. Most people that want to think in godly ways, when they recognize a wayward thought in their mind, do what they can to get rid of it. They "kick it out," so to speak, in order to not be thinking sinful thoughts. They might just stop thinking about it if they can, and if they cannot, they will try to think about something else. This "distracting" our minds might work to stop thinking a wrong thought; however, that is not the mighty way we pull down strongholds! Paul says we are supposed to handle that situation differently than just getting rid of wrong thoughts.

What does he say we are supposed to do? We are supposed to make that thought obey Christ! When we find a sinful thought rolling around in our heads, we are not supposed to kick it out. We are supposed to take it prisoner! We capture that thought. We say to our thought, "What are you thinking about? Oh, you are thinking about the topic of sex again, are you? Well, is your thought in line with God's Word? *No*? Well then, you just hold on a minute to see what I ought to do with you!" That thought is now in your possession; you have captured it. But do not let it go again until you have made it think properly! And how do we define properly? Thoughts that are proper are in line with what the Bible teaches us.

For instance, if I come across a woman who is "beautiful" according to the standards of the world, and I begin to dwell mentally on her physical attributes, what does taking my thought captive and making it obedient to Christ look like? It looks like this: I might think, "This woman is attractive according to the world's standards, but that doesn't mean she is beautiful. In order for me to know that, I would have to know more about her. Does she live a pure and chaste life like Peter said? Does she fear the Lord like what I read in Proverbs 31? Does she have a quiet and gentle spirit that God says is of great worth?" Do you see what I am doing? I am making my thought think in line with what the Bible teaches me about beauty. This could go even further if the woman in question is dressed immodestly. I could think about the proverb that speaks about an attractive woman that lacks discretion and how Solomon compares that situation to a pig with a gold ring in its nose (Proverbs 11:22). I might think that God expects me to keep my mind pure in spite of her provocative looks. The point is my mind is now thinking in line with what God's Word says about the thoughts running through my head.

I may even eventually come to the place where I do not concern myself with her beauty at all because her beauty is not something which ought to concern me.

The same process applies when my wife is too tired or when we have to wait for longer than normal to make love again. When sex was an idol to me, I would have thought those situations meant she does not like sex or she does not find me attractive. Maybe I would think that communicated that she does not even love me. When that thought is taken captive and made obedient to Christ, now I can think, "I know Judi loves me. She shows her love to me in more ways than just in the bedroom. She is tired and this is an opportunity for me to exercise patience." Maybe I might even think something like, "Even if she is snubbing me, I can still love her like Christ loves the church. Think of all the times I snub Him and yet He still loves me!" I can display love toward her that is Christlike instead of getting angry because of being self-centered.

Thinking biblically is what pulls down the strongholds. The more I do this, the more my mind is renewed, reprogrammed by the principles in God's Word instead of the standards in the world. The more I think thoughts that are obedient to Christ, the more my life is free from the devil's influence. If the devil is using my thoughts to tempt me, waging war with this weapon actually sends him packing!

Resist the devil and he will flee from you!
(James 4:7 NIV)

When he sends his fiery darts at me and I take those thoughts captive to make them obey Christ, they become a powerful weapon turned against him. His temptations ultimately lead me to think more in line with God's truth. His attempts at trying to deceive me make me think more biblically in the end! As a result, he quickly sees his attempts to deceive me are not only ineffective but also counter-productive. When I take my thoughts captive and make them obedient to Christ, his failed attempt to get me to sin just made me stronger in the Lord! And he certainly does not want that...so off he goes like a scolded little puppy with his tail between his legs. The more I win those battles like that, the less likely he is to keep hitting me in that area, knowing he is only making me stronger spiritually.

Yes, sir, the weapons that God has given us to fight this battle are mighty in God! If we would just be smart enough to utilize those weapons, we would see great victories in this area of our lives!

A Quick Recap

Let me wrap up by recapping a few things... Keeping Jesus as number one in your heart is imperative to getting the altar of your heart right for God. Jesus is number one! Seeing Him as your everything, more than that, your Only Thing, must be the foundation of this new altar you are building. Renewing our minds is the process in our renovation project which will ensure we have built a proper altar from which we can worship God acceptably. Thinking thoughts that are in line with the Scriptures forces our brains to stay on the right track and replaces the old idolatrous thoughts with new holy thoughts. A renewed mind helps prevent the devil from coming back to reclaim and defile the new altar we are building. Finally, the last step of putting on the new self created to be like Jesus in true righteousness and holiness is the way we offer up sacrifices on the new altar which are holy and acceptable to God. That is what we will discuss in our next chapter.

CHAPTER 8

THE NEW MAN

Put on the new man who is renewed in knowledge
according to the image of Him who created him.
—Colossians 3:10 NKJV

As I have previously disclosed, my idolatry concerning sex had negatively manifest itself in my relationship with Judi. But now that I had confessed and repented of my sinful perspective, we both could tell something was different. My repentance manifest itself in more ways than just tears. Remember, "Repentance isn't when you cry, it's when you change." There were plenty of tears, mind you, but there was much more. My mind was being renewed and my heart was being set right. Jesus was back on the throne where He belongs, and His Word had been restored as the basis for my thoughts. The great God who loves me and cares about me had done an amazing work in my heart and life. What an awesome God we serve! I began to experience the spiritual truth that when transformation occurs in the heart, it always shows up on the outside. Like Jesus said, "Clean the inside of the cup and the outside will become clean as well." All things associated with sex were no longer a matter of frustration and disappointment but opportunities to glorify God and show my love to my wife. And that perspective had changed in more areas than just sex. Now, everything in our relationship was an opportunity to be a God-honoring husband and express Christlike love to my wife.

A couple of months in and Judi said to me out of the blue, "I really like the new you!"

The new me? Hmm… I like that! She was right. There was a new element to who I had become as a husband. There was newness, not only in the level of importance sex had taken in my heart but also the way I approached all elements of my role as a husband. Judi's husband was not the same guy he was before. Funny how things can change like that! Paul teaches us that if anyone is in Christ, he is a new creation; the old goes away and newness comes to replace it (2 Corinthians 5:17). Well, for sure something was new for me.

Remember our litmus test for idolatry? You can tell if something has become an idol to a person if they are willing to sin to get it or if they sin when they do not get it. That dynamic had left our physical intimacy. I did not feel the need to manipulate her anymore. I would not try to "guilt her" into sex or get her to make promises for later that night. My thoughts about how things should go had changed. I did not expect my wife to be ready and willing for sex whenever I wanted. I could now appreciate that she is not the same as me in the libido department. Her sex drive was never as strong as mine and thinking it should be (or that if it wasn't meant she did not love me) was no longer a part of my perspective. Not only that, but when things do not go "as planned" (which still occurs regularly), my reaction is markedly different. Previously, I would feel rejected and offended; now I responded with understanding and patience. I could allow for her to be tired or not in the mood without it being a major affront to my manhood or a failure on her part as a woman.

These changes were a part of the process which this chapter hopes to highlight…putting on the new man which God has created us to be in Christ Jesus. I cannot say it enough, "Repentance is never complete until what God defines as right replaces the wrong which our sinful nature has produced in us." Remember the three-step process from Ephesians 4 that Paul outlined for us: (1) put off the old man; (2) be renewed in the spirit of your mind; and (3) put on the new man. That is God's plan of sanctification for the Christian. That is how we get to be more like Jesus.

My wife likes to use the analogy of working with pigs on a farm. It is date night but you have been out working with the pigs all week without ever once changing your clothes. Those clothes are nasty, stinky and soiled, ready for the incinerator! You do not even want to wear them into the house. Even the washing machine is no solution for these pig-stink saturated duds. Removing those nasty clothes, throwing them in the trash is putting off the old man. Step one is done. The clothes are gone, but you are still in desperate need of a shower! The smell is still lingering, stuck in your hair and on your skin. A long hot shower with lots of soap and scrubbing is like the renewing your mind portion of the process, cleaning things up and making them smell nice. The shower is over, and you are clean as a whistle, but there you are, standing there naked. You cannot go out like that. You have got to put on some clean clothes. You get suited up in your nicest clothes for date night. That is the putting on the new man part. You come out of the bathroom with the process complete and your wife looks at you and says, "Wow! You clean up nice!"

God's people always "clean up nice" when we walk the path of sanctification. The further down that path we walk, the more like Jesus we become. Disposing of old man behaviors and changing our thoughts is wrapped up nicely in a bow by putting on the new. So let's get to it!

New Man Stuff

There are so many ways we can put on the new man when recovering from sexual idolatry. Each of us have expressed our sexual idolatry differently, and so our new man clothes will look differently for us as individuals. You may have to address some different situations that I did not have to. I might have had to replace sinful behaviors you do not. Needless to say, I am aware that I will not be able to cover all the bases for everyone seeking to put on the new man, but I do want to stress the three big ones where the new me really showed up. The other areas I will trust to the Holy Spirit to work out in your life.

Area 1: No More Strings Attached

The first area of putting on the new man for me had to do with being able to show my love to Judi without strings attached. I am not talking about when we make love but rather the tangible ways throughout the day I express my love for her. I can now engage in acts of kindness toward her without thinking that it would be a favor she would later have to repay. When that sexual idol was present in my heart, it was regular for me to use things normal decent people do for one another as a tool to ensure she would be amicable in return. As I think back on this reality, I am ashamed at how many of my "loving expressions" or "kindnesses" were selfish intentions done as more of a down payment for expected future services. My idolatry had created a perspective in me that convinced me it was necessary to manipulate Judi in ways that would put her indebted to me. Because it was clear that she did not value sex as much as I did, I began to understand that she would not pursue it like I expected her to. If I felt it had been too long of a stretch since we last made love, I reasoned she needed a push in the right direction. That is when the manipulations would begin. The more "nice things" I did for her, the more I thought she would come to bed that night "in the mood." I would drop hints that I expected her to pick up on so she would understand my kindness should be responded to with an eagerness on her part to please me sexually. What a nitwit I was!

However, with that idol lying in a heap on the floor and a new altar set up in my heart, I was now free to do nice things without expectation of repayment! I could come home from work and offer to help with dinner without thinking she would be indebted to me. I would offer to cook or clean in order to help her out when her plate was full. (I am not sure I can rightfully describe my cooking as an act of kindness, but hey! It's the thought that counts!) If I left the room I could politely ask if she wanted me to get anything for her while I was up. All kinds of ways for me to be good toward her were freed up as a means available for me to demonstrate my love and appreciation. And because those things were free from the hooks of manipulation and indebtedness, they became actual acts of kindness! They were no longer counterfeit. I could tell, and so could she.

It felt good in my heart to know I could be nice without having to be reimbursed. I am sure my wife resented my previous manipulations, but she was not the only one that was negatively impacted by them. I also had an inner guilt knowing that I was mimicking kindness toward her for selfish reasons. I knew I was doing it. I knew that I would pretend to be selfless, when ultimately, at the heart of the matter I was being self-focused. But now that is all different. I became thankful to God for my wife and glad for opportunities to let her know I appreciated her. Most of the time my previous acts of kindness resulted in my disappointment because very rarely did they accomplish what I intended, but now I get to enjoy showing her I love her. I think she is glad for that new development as well!

Area 2: More Open and Honest Communication

Another new man reality for me is being able to talk more openly and without argument about our sex life. Because of our long-standing history of fighting about sex, this one carries with it the sense of great relief. In the past, any discussion about sex would lead to us fighting or end up with my wife in tears. She would not see it my way, and I could not see it hers. Back then, there was no solution for us that would resolve our issues. That is different now. As it pertains to sex, we are now able to discuss it without my idol whispering in my ear, telling me what to expect. I can ask her questions without expecting a certain answer or getting upset if I do not hear what I want to hear. I can ask her questions and want to know what she really thinks, you know, what her actual opinion is. Previously, I would not always openly share what was going on in my head, knowing it would probably just lead to an argument. As a result, I thought I had to keep it to myself and it would lead me to become more and more bitter about whatever was bothering me. That is different now. I am more open and honest when I am struggling or confused about sexual matters. This is a growing reality for us as we work out what all needs to be shared and what is unnecessary, but we are working it out without all the previous conflict. Even in the "working things out" department, it has the result of bringing us closer together. In short, I am communicating about sexual things better!

This better communication does not only occur in the bedroom behind closed doors. Across the board we can talk about anything better. The bitterness which originated in our bed used to seep its way into other areas of my communication with Judi. The fruit of frustration which used to grow on account of my sexual idolatry is no longer a regular experience for me. Therefore, I communicate in other areas of our life much more readily. I find myself asking for her to speak to me more about her day or her struggles. I no longer avoid it but like to listen when we speak about the details of her day. I used to think I had to do that "listening thing" for her to be interested in me later, but now it does not have that "later" element anymore. I genuinely do want to know how her day went, and I inquire about it.

I have always known that Judi likes to talk with me, but I am generally not a talker. Before, I would have to force myself to be emotionally present when she would speak with me. These days I get a little jealous if we do not have those types of conversations, so I purposefully ask her about things. I speak with her when she is talking instead of just being a silent observer in a one-sided "discussion." I have started to share what I am thinking when we speak about things, even things I used to feel were trivial. I think I figured it out that conversations are more than just using up your daily quota of words so you can go to bed verbally fulfilled! Now they are enjoyable experiences with the woman I love.

Remember back to our discussion (last chapter) about the purposes behind God inventing sex? In that section we saw that a big part of God's design was that sex would help create intimacy through our vulnerability. That reality is true in communication as well. The times past where we discussed our sex life were once opportunities for me to change Judi to get her more in line with my idol. Now I was free from that motive and able to be open and inquisitive. Those moments made me feel vulnerable, but because we could be honest and accepting of each other, they also helped build trust. That intimacy began to spill over into the other parts of our lives, especially our communication. I did not realize previously that my hesitance to "open up" in conversations was because I was short on trust.

Area 3: Devotions and Prayer

One of the worst things turning sex into an idol did to our marriage is that it caused our worship to be divided. My wife is sold out to glorifying and loving the Lord in every aspect of who she is. As a Christian woman, wife, and mother (as well as the many other hats she wears!), she is constantly looking for ways to honor Jesus. I was also convinced I had similar commitments. When God revealed the idolatry present in my heart, I began to see more and more that I had slipped away from my true devotion to Him. That is what idols do to us. And the reality of the situation was that Judi and I were not on the same page as we served the Lord. I was not only on a different page but also in the wrong book!

The regular sense of "lack of oneness" in our bedroom kept us divided in our relationship with God. As a result, for the most part she served God by herself, and I served Him by myself. (I remember times when Judi would specifically tell me that!) This lack of unity kept us from worshipping and seeking Him together. Talk about the devil robbing us of something precious! He is a such a thief! Our experience was that this idol kept us apart in the most crucial area of our life!

I have heard it said that each one of us must have their own individual relationship with Jesus. While I think that is true for most people, I am not so sure it is entirely true for married couples. Although I know each of us is responsible to keep seeking first the kingdom and His righteousness, I believe there is a unique situation for the Christians who get married where, when the two become one, they actually worship and serve Him together. When God develops a oneness and intimacy between a man and woman in marriage, they are now personally impacted by how their spouse is doing with Jesus. We receive the benefits of a spouse who loves Jesus but can also be negatively impacted when that same spouse is neglecting their walk with the Lord. We often quote Jesus's words at weddings where He said, "What God has joined together, let no man separate." I have for the longest time thought that instruction was given to people outside the marriage doing things that might lead one of them to break their marriage covenant. More and more I am seeing that Jesus was speaking to the married couple! A husband or a wife can think, speak, or act in ways that would separate the unity which Jesus creates as we do marriage His way. We are told not to do that. God has joined us together and sees the two of us as one. When I serve Him, I do not do it absent of my wife even if she is not present. The same is true for her.

The repentance and renewal which took place in our marriage has brought us to a place of rejoicing in what God has done for us. Things had been out of order for thirty years! And because it had been wrong for so long, the feeling of joy and thankfulness for things being made right overwhelmed our hearts! Our hearts being overwhelmed brought us both to a place of deeper worship for the Lord. We had both resigned ourselves to the idea that even though we both knew things were not everything God wanted them to be, it would be our "normal." I am so thankful that we were wrong about that. We have never been as close as we are now, and we serve Him together in a greater capacity.

Godly Character

Sexual idolatry prevents certain godly characteristics from being present in who we are as husbands. What are some "new man" clothes you can put on in your role as a husband that sexual idolatry had prevented from being there? Maybe like me, your previous kindnesses came with strings attached. Maybe you used to be a closed book in how you communicated with your wife. Maybe there was a distance in your heart toward her that prevented unity in seeking the Lord together. Those things can change as we dress ourselves in our new clothes. Whatever the new clothes are which you need to put on, do it. Dress yourself in "true righteousness and holiness" in your role as a husband just as the Bible directs you.

If you do not see any areas where the "new you" needs to show up, pray and ask the Lord. He will direct you. He loves to answer those sorts of prayers! All too often He hears us praying about worldly things: jobs, health, finances, freedom from struggles, you know, things that have to do with Him making our lives easier for us. Very rarely do we pray for the right type of things—holiness in our character, the ability to be more like Christ, to endure all things in a way that brings Him glory. Let Him know you really want to be the kind of man He wants your wife to be married to. Ask Him for ways you can show her His kind of love. Be prepared to get stretched beyond what is normal or natural to your personality. Do not think you are such an old dog you cannot learn any new tricks! God sees what is lacking and is more than happy to not only point it out but also to help you become the husband you ought to be.

And here is a novel thought: do not be opposed to allowing your wife the opportunity to point some of those things out too! After all, she is your God-given helper. God has placed her in your life in a unique position no one else holds. I always say, "Men that do not seek out and consider their wife's opinion shoot themselves in the foot." She is right there close by you and may know you better than just about anybody else on earth. Your wife can provide insight for you that no one else has. You neglect an incredible asset when you do not seek out your wife's perspective on things!

In all my years of ministering to married couples, I have not come across too many wives who are unwilling to share their insights with their husbands. They are glad for the opportunity to let you know what they see. They may not always do it in the wisest way, but most of them want to share their perspectives with their husbands. Unfortunately, the opposite is true. I have found many husbands who do not value the opinion of their wife, especially if her opinion has to do with some defect or shortcoming which might be present in them. It is a sad situation when a man does not value the perspective of his wife. This situation often develops because of our past idolatry. It can create in us a contempt for her worth, especially if she has been a "nonparticipant" in our idol worship. This is a "new man" opportunity for you. Learn to value your wife. Let her know you value her. Let her know how foolish it was for you to belittle or ignore her opinions. And do what you can to show her that from now on, things are going to be different in that area!

There are lots of opportunities available to Christian men for us to learn how to be better at our jobs as husbands. There are men's retreats, marriage seminars, books and tapes on the subject, and much more. Many churches have ministries which are specifically focused on those areas of a man's life. Part of the "new man" approach to your role as a husband is to put yourself in a position to become better and better at your job.

Often, we do not know our roles because of a couple reasons. First, because this "Christlike husband" gig does not come easy to us. Being a Christlike husband is not something that flows naturally from our humanity, and it is always a heavy burden when we try to figure it out on our own. If it has been hard for you, be encouraged by what Jesus said to those who were following Him.

> Come to me, all you who are weary and burdened, and I will give you rest. Take my yoke upon you and learn from me, for I am gentle and lowly in heart, and you will find rest for your souls. For my yoke is easy and my burden is light. (Matthew 11:28–30 NIV)

The hard work of being like Jesus can wear us out if we do it alone. Becoming like Christ happens as we are yoked together with Him. He wants the closeness of our relationship with Him to be instructive to who we are as Christian men and Christian husbands. It makes sense. To be like Christ, we must hang out with Him a lot. We have got to learn it from Him being next to us, working on this whole "Christlike husband" thing together. When we are yoked together with Him is when the learning takes place. It is when we are in the saddle together that His character begins to rub off on us.

Another reason we do not know our roles well is because we have not always had good examples to follow. The other men in our lives that are husbands are not always the best role models. Even our own fathers have not always shown us that they were good at loving our moms. Not having a good role model is kind of like dumping all the pieces of a puzzle on the table and then throwing away the lid. The lid has the picture on it of what it is all supposed to look like when the puzzle is completed. If we do not know what it is supposed to look like when it is all said and done, we will find it extremely difficult to make any progress at all in figuring out the puzzle. We will often throw up our hands in defeat and give up on the whole idea of even doing the puzzle. Having a good role model does not always ensure those who see them will turn out just like them, but it sure can help us do our jobs better if we know what things are supposed to look like!

One more reason we do not know our roles very well is because it requires much of us. Being a good husband requires us to be unselfish, able to deny ourselves, and make sacrifices. It requires us to take up our cross and die to ourselves. Not many men are willing to pay that price. Unfortunately, that means we are not only going to do our job as a husband poorly but that we will not be true disciples of Jesus. He told us we could not be His disciples if we will not deny ourselves, take up our cross, and follow Him daily. Thankfully, He can transform that in us! The new man who we are in Christ is an unselfish, self-denying, self-sacrificing cross carrying disciple of Jesus! We are different at the core. And when we are different at the core, that changes everything, including who we are as husbands.

I want to close this chapter by reminding you of Paul's words to the Christians in Corinth:

> Therefore, if anyone is in Christ, he is a new creation; old things have passed away, behold, all things have become new! (2 Corinthians 5:17 NKJV)

I echo Paul's sentiments and say wholeheartedly, "Amen and amen!"

CHAPTER 9

To God Be the Glory!

I beseech you therefore, brethren, by the mercies of
God, that you present your bodies a living sacrifice, holy,
acceptable to God, which is your reasonable service.

—Romans 12:1 NKJV

When I first became a Christian, my life was turned upside down! Jesus forgave me for some incredibly nasty sins, and He had to contend with the total wreck I had made of my life. Talk about a major renovation project! I was messed up! But messed up as I was, He got right to work and changed things left and right. I experienced the transformation only His Holy Spirit can bring to a wasted life. I knew I was pretty screwed up, and because of that, Jesus had a ton of work to do. This often made me feel terrible about myself and what I had become. I wished my life were not as messed up as it was so God would not have had to forgive me for so much.

At the beginning in my walk with the Lord, I sometimes wrestled with the thought of why God waited so long to save me. I inwardly wished that I had not wasted the early years of my life in self-centered sinful living. The more I served Jesus, the more I realized I missed out on many opportunities to serve God and share Him with others. I inwardly wondered why God did not send someone to share the Gospel message with me sooner. I *just knew* that I could have been a better Christian if I had become one earlier in life. These types of emotions spread in my heart and began to get directed toward others. I often got resentful toward people who, after I got saved, I found out were Christians. I was upset at them for not telling me about Jesus when I was lost. I knew full well how wicked and sinful I became as I went through life without Jesus Christ as my Savior and Lord, and in a weird way, I kind of blamed other Christians for the person I had become!

It probably will not surprise you to learn that living without Jesus led to me make some pretty bad decisions! My choices revealed the self-centeredness of my heart and expressed that selfishness in rotten ways. When someone told me about Jesus and the Gospel, I had a lot to repent for because I was the wretch mentioned in the hymn "Amazing Grace." It bothered me that I had been as bad as I was.

Then I came across this passage in Luke 7 when Jesus was invited to have dinner with a Pharisee named Simon. The visit was going fine until a local woman found out Jesus was in town. When she learned He was there, this sinful woman came in and began weeping at Jesus's feet. She used her tears to wash His feet and, afterward, her hair to wipe them dry. She kissed His feet and perfumed them and then kissed them some more! It was her way of demonstrating her great love to Jesus for forgiving her for such a sinful life.

The whole time Simon and his guests were inwardly judging the entire scene. Before this woman interrupted their meal, Simon had thoughts that Jesus was perhaps a prophet or a great man of God. But now he knew that his previous assessment of Jesus must have been wrong. If He really were a prophet, Jesus would most definitely know that this woman was not someone you permit to touch you. She was so sinful that just being near her would defile Him. A prophet would know such things!

However, Jesus was more than just a prophet, and He could read Simon's thoughts. Then He corrected those wrong thoughts by telling him a story that went something like this: There was a moneylender who loaned out money to two different people: one a ton of money and the other a few bucks. This moneylender then found it in his heart to cancel both debts, the enormous debt as well as the miniscule one. Jesus then asks Simon, "Which of those two people who had their debts canceled would love the moneylender more? Which one of them would be more grateful for him forgiving their debt?" Simon was smart enough to know that the one who had the bigger debt would be the more grateful, and he told Jesus as much.

> "You have judged correctly," Jesus said. Then He turned toward the woman and said to Simon, "Do you see this woman? I came into your house. You did not give me any water for my feet, but she wet my feet with her tears and wiped them with her hair. You did not give me a kiss, but this woman from the time I entered, has not stopped kissing my feet. You did not put oil on my head, but she has poured perfume on my feet. Therefore, I tell you, her many sins have been forgiven—as her great love has shown. But whoever has been forgiven little loves little."
> (Luke 7:43–47 NIV)

Simon did not know what it was like to be forgiven much, but this woman did. The reason she did is because before she met Jesus, her life was full of sin. Jesus came into her life, forgave her sins, and cleaned house. Her sins were great, but God's grace was greater. That reality led her to love Him very much! Enough to weep over His feet, wash them with her hair, and kiss them repeatedly.

There is no telling what my life would have been like if I came to know Jesus at a younger age. Those answers are lost in the eternal ramifications of the "what if" section of the past. My personal history can never be altered. However, this one thing I know: my debts have been canceled too! Just like the first debtor of Jesus's parable, my many sins have been forgiven! Jesus paid the price for my sins on the cross of Calvary. He was tortured and crucified on account of those sins. His blood was shed so I could be washed clean. Because He had much to forgive, I have much to be thankful for. And I love Jesus so much more for that! Not that I am thankful for how sinful I was, but I am thankful for how patient and compassionate and merciful and loving my God is. I intimately know those things about God on account of my many sins.

I approach my struggle with sexual idolatry from a similar perspective. I wish this had not been such a problem for our marriage for as long as it was. I wish my heart were not so sinful that it would pervert something which God created to bless us into something that brought ruin and misery for so many years. I could spend all kinds of mental energy delving into the "what ifs" surrounding this issue or what things could have been like if this idol were demolished earlier, and I realize that I can never know what would have been if things had changed earlier. But this I do know: the gratitude in my heart for being free from my sexual idolatry is so overwhelming. The forgiveness I have received from God and from Judi for my terrible sin is so valuable to me. I love God so much for being gracious with His forgiveness. I love Judi so much for being like God in forgiving me. I am so thankful for the blessings that have come on account of their forgiveness granted to me. I am so thankful for the change. If I had not been a prisoner to that idol for so long, I would not relish in my freedom as much as I do.

This experience testifies to my heart of how wonderful my God is. Jesus is amazing. He deserves all the glory for being the Gideon in my story. He tore down that idol and helped me build a new altar in my heart, one on which I can lay down my life and say, "Have Your way with me, O Lord! I am Yours forever!"

CHAPTER 10

A WIFE'S JOURNEY

This chapter is written by my wife Judi in order to give you her perspective concerning the sexual frustrations our marriage experienced as the result of my sexual idolatry. We decided it would be helpful for you as the reader, to understand some of what our wives endure when we as husbands do not have our hearts right concerning sexual things. Knowing our wife's perspective and some of the pains it causes them may be useful to bring us the conviction necessary to repent of sexual idolatry. I encourage you as a Christian husband to learn about the pain your own sexual idolatry may have caused your wife. Seek her out. Ask her to share her side of the story with you. Really let her know you are sorry for the pain you caused her. And most of all, seek her forgiveness. Be patient with her healing as she works through the damage your sin may have caused her. And pray for her regularly for God to undo the damages your sin has inflicted on her. God is a compassionate, merciful, forgiving and healing God. He can and will forgive your sin and bring healing to your marriage bed. Very often, He takes time to do that work instead of doing it in an instance. He knows which method we need most and always does things His way for our good and His glory. Exercise patience as God does the healing work in your wife necessary to transform your marriage. With that in mind, read on and get a glimpse into a wife's journey.

I want to tell you the story of my journey as a believer in Christ, wife, pastor's wife, mother, and friend. I am writing this so that you may see the real struggles I have experienced on my journey. I have had pain and difficulty that I was often not allowed to share because of the different "hats" I wear. However, my prayer is that at the end of this journey there will be victory, glory to God, and restored relationships that can be stronger and more glorious than ever before.

I was a product of domestic abuse. My childhood experience was filled with pain and abuse. I got married when I was eighteen, and looking back from where I am now, I know I was always looking for a way of escape. My marriage was no different. It was a means of escape.

I met the Lord one night a little more than a year before I was married. I had recently lost a fiancée to a car accident. He was supposed to be my savior. The loss was so much more to me as I thought he was my way out. When that did not happen, my depressed state spiraled down more than before, and the only option I saw before me was to end it all. My plan was that October night to slit my wrist and it would all be over. All the pain would be gone. Little did I know, God had other plans! As I lightly traced my wrist with the razor blade, slowly working up to the final deed, a drop of blood fell on a Bible that sat at my feet. I picked it up, and as I opened it, the words from Luke 12:20 NIV jumped out at me!

> You Fool! This very night your life will be demanded from you.

I can barely explain what happened next. I remember how in an instant I knew God was there, and that He was real! He saw me! And He was calling me a fool for wanting to take my life. I fell to my knees and cried out to God, "If You want my life, take it! Because I do not want it anymore."

And guess what? He did!

My life spiraled out of control and one thing after another unfolded in my life. Not realizing what was happening, I tried to keep up. One minute I was living at home going about life "normally," the next I was in a foster home. Soon afterward I was running away and moving from house to house, not knowing where I belonged. I began going to church for real and officially began my journey with God. I am amazed at how God orchestrated it all and how He knew exactly the people to bring into my life along the way.

This all leads me to my marriage to Michael. I imagined it was going to be great. My husband was great. He was patient, he was kind, and he was funny. On the other hand, I was manipulative, angry, selfish, and damaged, coming in with a lot of baggage. This made for a rough first eight years. There were a lot of arguing and fights on account of me and my baggage. Michael would not argue back or talk much. He would usually just say, "It takes two to argue and I'm not going to argue with you." This usually provoked me to even more anger!

Our sexual relationship started while we were dating. We were not Christians at the time and so we just did what was normal to us. Michael became a Christian shortly after we began dating and decided that sex before marriage did not honor God, and so he stopped sleeping with me. The abuse I endured as a child taught me to believe that sex was how you showed someone that you loved them. When we're married, I was happy to resume our sexual relationship; after all, that was how I knew for sure that my husband loved me.

Part of being discipled and going to church included learning about a different kind of love. I began to see how the significance I had placed on sex was bad, and consequently I began to understand sex as dirty and bad. This realization created a new problem. Now I did not want to have sex anymore because I did not think it was good. I was like a pendulum that had just swung from one extreme to the complete opposite. I began seeking advice concerning this issue from the godly women in my life. I heard anything from "You just have to do it" to "Anything goes in marriage" to "Do whatever you want." Some women I talked to barely ever had sex and very few actually enjoyed it (that was rare). I continued to seek advice as I was desperate to know what was right. Through the years I think I read every Christian book printed on the subject.

I really wanted to love my husband the right way. I eventually realized on this journey I was having trouble loving those around me. I did not know why until God showed me. Michael and I had been married about eight years and I begged God to help me love my husband and four children. One day He revealed to me that I had a darkness in my heart that prevented me from loving like I wanted to. He showed me I had hate—a deep-rooted bitterness toward people who had hurt me in my past. He showed me clearly one day that I could not love—not my husband, not my children, and not even God Himself if I did not let go of the hate in my heart. My heart had to change. I had to let God deal with the sins of those people who hurt me and transfer the debt I knew they owed me to Him. I had to hand it over to Jesus and not let that darkness rule my heart anymore. If I would not, I would not be able to love. This struggle within me took about two weeks. I wrestled through the emotions and pain, but in the end, I trusted God and transferred it all to Him. The pain of my past was now His to deal with as He saw fit, and as a result, I was free!

I cannot describe for you the freedom that came at that time, but I can say that at that moment there was a great weight lifted off my heart and I could see my family in a new light.

Even though I had found this new freedom, sex was still a major area of contention in our marriage. For many years I was not very compliant and very often rejected my husband's advances. This caused many fights. Things were not right. It took a long time for me before I came to the conclusion that sex was a good thing which God had created married people to enjoy, and that according to Him, it was an important part of our relationship. Once I realized this, I knew I needed to have sex more frequently with Michael. At this point, sex became a "chore" for me, something I just had to do. On some occasions I would enjoy it, but for the most part it was something I simply required myself to do. It was my duty.

I really want to say that my husband is a kind and patient man. He is a fun and loving father. Michael has had to endure a great deal in our marriage on account of my struggles. He loved me the best he could in the situation he was in. For the most part, he cared for me and acted lovingly toward me. He was thoughtful and tried to love me like Christ in most areas of our relationship. All in all, we really got along well through the years, but there was always this one thing between us. Sex was an idol for him.

As the years went on, I noticed a pattern emerging in our marriage. As the mother of nine, running a house, homeschooling, managing all our home's finances and his business finances, as well as church and many other things, I realized that we only had one thing we really fought about—and that was sex. Our sex life was still an area of contention. If I was exhausted after a long day and happened to say no, I might get the cold shoulder for the next couple days. Very often I would also have an overwhelming sense of guilt. For years I cried out over and over for God to fix this in our marriage so we would not have this struggle. I did not find the answers and I did not know where to look.

I had spoken to my husband on and off about going for counseling. I thought talking to someone outside the situation might help. He would say it would not do any good and that we should be able to work it out by ourselves. Since we were counselors, he reasoned that we should be able to counsel ourselves as if we were counseling someone else and resolve the issue. These discussions always ended in a heated disagreement. We just could not seem to come to any resolution concerning our problems in the bedroom. It was usually determined in the end that the problem was all mine and that I needed to "fix" me. Apparently, I just needed to enjoy it more and then it would be better. Or I needed to want it more and pursue sex with him more often, you know, show some desire for it. He would often explain that he did not feel I was attracted to him or that I wanted to have sex with him. He had an idea in his head of what sex was supposed to be like and I could not live up to it. I just could not seem to get it right.

I did not pursue any of those solutions. I was growing to hate sex. I reasoned that if we did not have to have sex, our marriage would be amazing. I thought many times, "God has to have something better than this in mind for us," but I could not figure out how to get there. There were so many times when I counseled other couples and I would tell them, "God has so much good for your marriage. It will be amazing," all the while longing for that reality to be true in this area of our marriage.

Twenty-seven years into marriage, after another fight about sex, I was again crying out to the Lord, begging for help. I was begging for God to change me and my heart in this area of our life. I heard the still small voice: "Are you willing to go forward with me alone?" In an instant I knew in my heart what that meant. God was asking me if I was willing to grow in Him and learn from Him, leaving behind my husband and children if that was what was necessary for me to go deeper with Him. I said yes.

I dove into the Word of God headfirst, with no looking back. I began this part of my journey waking every morning saying, "Your life is not your own. You were bought with a price." I studied the Word to see how God wanted me to change and grow. I looked for every opportunity to serve Him. What I learned in the next few years is a book all its own, but one thing I can tell you is that it was another step of me being free in Christ. More of my burdens lifted that day and I was ready and excited for what was to come next. I studied books of the Bible. I studied my biblical counseling training materials with the intention of applying it to my own life. I soon discovered the most challenging areas to apply God's commands were in my own home with my children and husband. But I was determined to honor God the best I could in everything, continually searching for how to do that and what it looked like.

That also included fulfilling my "duty" in the area of sex. At this point it was still a duty, an act of obedience. Because I loved God and wanted to please Him, I would have sex with Michael. Often, beforehand, I would pray that God would help me to enjoy it and that my husband would be pleased in it. Sometimes I did enjoy it. I did my best to do what God said. I would not say no as often as I used to, and I sought to please him in this area. The problem now was he was still not pleased. Once in a while there would be some short-term contentment, but that never lasted long.

During that time, I really recognized a distance between us. I realized we were not friends. There was a big gap which separated us and a great deal more missing from our relationship than I ever realized. There was little to no spiritual relationship between us. I did not like that feeling, and so I began praying that my husband would become my friend, that he would be the person I wanted to go to. I loved him, but there was something missing. We were not whole.

Our thirtieth anniversary was coming up, and because we had never had a honeymoon, we started to plan one. The plan was that we would go on a tropical vacation for two weeks. Everything was in motion, and because I am the perpetual planner, I started thinking of ways to work on "us" while we were there. We would have lots of alone time together and I thought we could read and pray and work on our relationship.

Shortly before our trip we had another big fight. It had been building for some time. I had a physical health issue that was preventing us from having any physical relations. I was so hurt by this fight. The pain was strong. I again was crying out and begging for God's help and wisdom. There was a day that I was lamenting over this area of our lives, begging God to tell me what to do. With my Bible in front of me looking for answers, I read every instruction on sex in the Scriptures I could find to see what I was doing wrong. Then it came again. His still small voice said, "I am pleased with you in this area. You are not doing anything wrong. He is."

Another stepping-stone along the journey! Another huge weight lifted! More freedom came! That day I believed what God said. This meant I did not have to feel guilty. This meant that if my husband got mad that it was not my bubble of concern. His problem was between him and God. If he got mad, I did not have to spend the next few days trying to figure it out. It was not my problem to fix. I could have a good day and not lose sleep over it. I was freed from the guilt and shame I was feeling.

We had a great honeymoon! The trip was awesome. Of course, we could have sex whenever we wanted, so my husband was happy the entire trip. We enjoyed ourselves and our time together. I was still seeking God because I knew there was still something missing in our relationship. It grieved my heart and I would speak with God often about it in the mornings. However, I pushed it back so we could enjoy our time away together.

A downward spiral began after our trip. We had another family trip shortly after our getaway. This trip did not go as well. On account of the freedom I had found in knowing I was honoring God, I was not being hindered by my husband's frustrations of not getting what he wanted when he wanted it. The boat began to rock. He spent a good portion of this trip angry with me. We mainly just avoided each other for a couple weeks. When we got back home, his frustration seemed to escalate. His irritation grew. He got very cold and distant. I continued to pray and refused to let it negatively impact me or how I went about my day.

Then it happened. It was a Wednesday night and my husband had gone to teach Bible study. I stayed home with my younger girls and went to bed. I was almost asleep when he came in. He woke me up to tell me he had watched pornography the night before. He said he had to tell me because the conviction was too much. My mind was reeling. This was a way bigger deal for me than just messing up once and watching porn. He knew the impact pornography had on me in my life growing up and how I despised it. I got up, got dressed, and left. I went to be with God, and I cried my eyes out. I did not know what the future would be. I could not even think about what to read or say to God, so I just opened to the Psalms and started reading. I came back in around 1:00 a.m. and went to bed. I always say life changes on a dime. I was now standing on that dime.

The next day I got up as usual, going through my normal routine, trying to put on a face for my kids. It just so happened that day that some close friends had come by and we were talking in my shop. My husband came home from work early and found us there. He sat down to join us, and without warning, he confessed his failing to them. I felt like I had just been sucker punched. I still had not had time to process everything. I did not know what any of this meant or where it was going. He was a pastor, teacher, counselor, and father. I did not know how his sin would impact all these things or all these people. I was still reeling at this point, so I did the only thing I knew how to do: dive into the Word to desperately seek the wisdom I needed!

Each day was a day of uncertainty about the future. I could not discern my husband's response or decisions at this point. My future would be affected by His choices. I did not like being in this position and quickly had to switch to a more eternal perspective. I thought, "God works all things together for good for those who love Him… and so God is going to work this for good in our lives." I had to have that hope. I knew no matter how it turned out, it would be what God thought was best for me and my family.

Michael kept saying he was sorry. I could see he felt bad about what happened. He was giving me space and time. It was hard to talk to him. I knew what I wanted to say would hurt him and make him feel worse than he already did. However, even though I knew he felt bad, I also I knew it was not time to grant forgiveness. I could not do it yet. I was hurting, but I was also doubtful. He was sorry, but for what? For watching porn? For having to tell me? There was an acknowledgment that what he did was sin. There was confession to me and others that he had sinned. But there was not the repentance which told me it was going to be different now. In my mind, his remorse and sadness were not enough.

At one point I remember going to Michael, telling him I was not going to fix this for him. He had to do this. He had to do the work and make the change. He had to decide what that was going to look like. One of the hardest parts was that as a pastor's wife, counselor, mother of nine, who was I to talk to about this? Who could I go to discuss our situation without making him look bad? Who could I get godly counsel from? It was tough. Many people look up to him and respect him. I read so much during those days. My heart's desire was that I would honor God the best I could in this difficult situation.

To some it might seem that one incident with pornography is not a big deal, but for me it brought up so much of the abuse from my past. I now had questions in my head about my husband I never wanted to be there. It broke a trust I spent a lifetime working with God to develop. I still wrestled with the hurts from my past and now I had to keep those thoughts in check. I had a battle in my mind with awful thoughts I did not want to be there. That one incident created a lot more chaos in me than it might for someone else. It was an invisible line in the sand that I had drawn a long time ago that he was not allowed to cross. But now he crossed that line and I had to determine what that meant. I also had to give him some time in order to see what his response to it all would be. Each day that went by was difficult, and I was not sure how long I should wait for him to figure it out. How many days could I pretend everything was okay? Counseling, teaching Bible studies, going to church…because of this situation, now it all felt so fake.

I sought God and His Word for wisdom and direction each day. Robert Jones did a teaching called "Rebuilding after Betrayal" that helped me greatly. I walked through this teaching, applying things I learned as I went: guarding my heart from bitterness, preparing myself to stand ready to forgive, praying for my husband as he wrestled this out, all the while daily walking in the promise found in the Scripture: *"and we know that for those who love God all things work together for good"* (Romans 8:28a ESV, emphasis mine). I knew that He would use this for good no matter how it played out. He would use it for my good to make me more like Christ if I stayed pliable in my heart, allowing Him to mold me. I could not determine the outcome for my husband, but I could hope in Christ that the same would be true for him, that he would be transformed by this in a good way. That was my prayer.

Michael had begun meeting with a counselor. We also sat down and had a discussion with our co-pastor and his wife, letting them know what had happened and how we were struggling. Even though he was willing to, it was agreed between them and the counselor that since this was only a one-time thing that he would not have to step down as a pastor. However, we all agreed he would be required to do counseling and take steps to instill accountability.

After a few meetings he had with the counselor, Michael and I sat down to talk. Up to this point, we had not had very many discussions. I had some things I felt I needed to say. I did not want to say them because I knew it would hurt him to hear how badly he had hurt me, but I knew I needed to say what was on my heart. We sat down and I shared how hard this all had been for me and that I felt like he somehow blamed me for it all. At that point he interrupted me and said he had to share something with me. He had an assignment from his counselor which he wanted to read to me.

The counselor had asked him to answer the question "How has your turning sex into an idol affected your marriage?" The answer he read was "I blamed my wife." As he said those words, he broke. He began sobbing and telling me that all these years he blamed me for all our sexual problems. He had been convinced that our problems in the bedroom were all my fault. All this time he thought he was right, but now he knew how wrong he was. Through his tears, he said, "I have robbed you of thirty years and I can never give that back. I thought I loved you and that you did not love me enough. Now I know it was me that did not love you enough."

As crazy as it sounds, in that moment as he sat there sobbing, I felt like dancing. I wanted to get up and shout for joy! I was so excited to see the work which God had done—the brokenness I could see in my husband. I had a renewed hope for our relationship that now things could be different. The shackles that had held me since I was a child were breaking away.

In that moment I granted him forgiveness and boy, was he grateful! The years of pain he had caused us was all washing away as he repented, and I forgave him. This experience put us on a new road of healing. It felt like we were starting over. Our relationship felt brand-new. We spent the next few weeks doing a lot of talking and reading and rebuilding. Talking through the hard things. Reading God's perspective in a new light. Talking about what God desired our love life to be instead of what we wanted it to be. It took time but eventually we were able to come together again.

I knew our relationship was now restored and it would be better than ever before. Things are incredibly better even though we both still have work to do. God is not finished but has promised to continue the work in us until it is complete. We are committed to God and each other and are striving to please God in our relationship in a new way. We are still on guard in our hearts against idols that try to move on to the thrones of our hearts, but as we keep our eyes on Jesus, He helps us to tear them down.

I am truly thankful that God makes all things new and that the "all things" includes even our marriages! He has set us free!

ABOUT THE AUTHOR

Michael Ryan was saved by the grace of God in 1988 at the age of nineteen. He has enjoyed being a child of God for over thirty-two years! Redeemed from a sinful lifestyle including the occult, alcohol, and drugs, he has been involved in ministry for over thirty years. Opportunities to serve in advancing God's kingdom have included children's ministries, missions, teaching, preaching, pastoring, and counseling. He has authored two books on relationships and has been teaching on that subject for over twenty-five years. Michael has pastored in three different churches and is currently serving the Lord as co-pastor of the church in Potter Hollow located in Potter Hollow, New York. Michael has been married to his wife, Judi, for thirty-two years and is the father of five daughters, four sons and grandfather to one granddaughter with hopes of many more to come!

CPSIA information can be obtained
at www.ICGtesting.com
Printed in the USA
LVHW030751090721
692197LV00004B/453